DIRECTORS IN PERSPECTIVE

General editor: Christopher Innes

Jacques Copeau

What characterizes modern theatre above all is continual stylistic innovation, in which theory and presentation have combined to create a wealth of new forms – naturalism, expressionism, epic theatre, and so forth – in a way that has made directors the leading figures rather than dramatists. To a greater extent than is perhaps generally realized, it has been directors who have provided dramatic models for playwrights, though of course there are many different variations in this relationship. In some cases a dramatist's themes challenge a director to create new performance conditions (Stanislavski and Chekhov), or a dramatist turns director to formulate an appropriate style for his work (Brecht); alternatively a director writes plays to correspond with his theory (Artaud), or creates communal scripts out of exploratory work with actors (Chaikin, Grotowski). Some directors are identified with a single theory (Craig), others give definite shape to a range of styles (Reinhardt); the work of some has an ideological basis (Stein), while others work more pragmatically (Bergman).

Generally speaking, those directors who have contributed to what is distinctly "modern" in today's theatre stand in much the same relationship to the dramatic texts they work with, as composers do to librettists in opera. However, since theatrical performance is the most ephemeral of the arts and the only easily producible element is the text, critical attention has tended to focus on the playwright. This series is designed to redress the balance by providing an overview of selected directors' stage work: those who helped to formulate modern theories of drama. Their key productions have been reconstructed from promptbooks, reviews, scene-designs, photographs, diaries, correspondence and – where these productions are contemporary – documented by first-hand description, interviews with the director, and so forth. Apart from its intrinsic interest, this record allows a critical perspective, testing ideas against practical problems and achievements. In each case, too, the director's work is set in context by indicating the source of his ideas and their influence, the organization of his acting company, and his relationship to the theatrical or political establishment, so as to bring out wider issues: the way theatre both reflects and influences assumptions about the nature of man and his social role.

Christopher Innes

TITLES IN THIS SERIES

Ingmar Bergman: Lise-Lone and Frederick J. Marker
Joseph Chaikin: Eileen Blumenthal
Jacques Copeau: John Rudlin
Edward Gordon Craig: Christopher Innes
Max Reinhardt: John Styan
Peter Stein: Michael Patterson

FUTURE TITLES

André Antoine: Jean Chothia
Adolphe Appia: Richard Beacham
Jean-Louis Barrault: Thomas Bishop
Roger Blin: Odette Aslan and Ruby Cohn
Bertholt Brecht: John Fuegi
Peter Brook: Albert Hunt and Geoffrey Reeves
Jerzy Grotowski: Nicholas Sales
Tyrone Guthrie: Ronald Bryden
Constantin Stanislavski: Peter Holland
Giorgio Strehler: David Hirst
Andrzej Wajda: Maciej Karpinski

Jacques Copeau by Berthold Mahn

Jacques Copeau

JOHN RUDLIN
University of Exeter

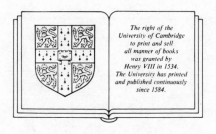

The right of the
University of Cambridge
to print and sell
all manner of books
was granted by
Henry VIII in 1534.
The University has printed
and published continuously
since 1584.

CAMBRIDGE UNIVERSITY PRESS

CAMBRIDGE
LONDON   NEW YORK   NEW ROCHELLE
MELBOURNE   SYDNEY

Published by the Press Syndicate of the University of Cambridge
The Pitt Building, Trumpington Street, Cambridge CB2 1RP
32 East 57th Street, New York, NY 10022, USA
10 Stamford Road, Oakleigh, Melbourne 3166, Australia

First published 1986

Printed in Great Britain at
the University Press, Cambridge

British Library Cataloguing in Publication Data
Rudlin, John
Jacques Copeau. – (Directors in perspective)
1. Theatrical producers and directors – France
– Biography   2. Copeau, Jacques
I. Title   II. Series
792'.0233'0924   PN2658.C74

Library of Congress Cataloguing in Publication Data
Rudlin, John.
Jacques Copeau.
(Directors in perspective)
Bibliography: p.
Includes index.
1. Copeau, Jacques, 1879–1940. 2. Theater – Production
and direction. I. Title. II. Series.
PN2638.C74R8   1986 792'.0233'0924   85–21339

ISBN 0 521 25305 5 hard covers
ISBN 0 521 27303 X paperback

to Thomas and Beryl

Contents

List of illustrations   *page* xi
Preface   xiii
Acknowledgements   xvii
1   Dramatic renovation   1
2   The text   24
3   The enemy of the theatre   36
4   The naked stage   51
5   Two presentations   64
6   Retreat in Burgundy   82
7   The new *commedia*   95
8   A popular theatre?   111
Appendix: *Chronological list of Copeau's productions*   125
Notes   130
Select bibliography   137
Index   139

Illustrations

Jacques Copeau by Berthold Mahn. DACS *frontispiece*

1	Reading in the garden at Limon, summer 1913. FC	*page* 11
2	Rehearsal of *L'Avare* at Limon, summer 1913. FC	12
3	Suzanne Bing as Olivia in *La Nuit des Rois*, drawn by Berthold Mahn. DACS	17
4	Louis Jouvet as Sir Andrew Aguecheek in *La Nuit des Rois*. FC	19
5	Drawing of Jouvet as Aguecheek by Mahn. DACS	20
6	Scene from *La Nuit des Rois*. FC	21
7	Drawing of a scene from *La Nuit des Rois* by Berthold Mahn. DACS	22
8	Neutral mask made by Diane Green (as used by the author in acting classes at the University of Exeter). Photograph: Steve Berry.	47
9	Théâtre de l'Athénée St-Germain, 1912. FC	53
10	The 1913 conversion of the Vieux-Colombier by Francis Jourdain. FC	54
11	Schematic drawing of cubes reproduced from *Registres III* (Gallimard *NRF*) by permission of Marie-Hélène Dasté.	56
12	Louis Jouvet in front of his model of the Garrick Theatre. FC	57
13	Louis Jouvet's 1919 conversion of the Vieux-Colombier. FC	58
14	Jouvet's *tryptique* for *Le Pacquebot Tenacity*. FC	66–7
15	Drawing by Jean Dulac of a scene in Act 2 of *Le Pacquebot Tenacity*. DACS	68
16	Scene in Act 1 of *Le Pacquebot Tenacity*, drawn by Jean Dulac.	69
17	The *tréteau* on the Garrick stage. FC	74
18	The *tréteau* on the Vieux-Colombier stage. FC	74
19	Jacques Copeau as Scapin, FC	75
20	Drawing by Jean Dulac of Louis Jouvet as Géronte in *Les Fourberies de Scapin*. DACS	76
21	Copeau as Scapin, drawn by Dulac. DACS	76
22	The logo of the Vieux-Colombier.	94
23	The Fratellini Brothers in their dressing-room. Courtesy of Annie Fratellini.	98
24	Jean Dasté as César. DC	102
25	Michel Saint-Denis as Knie. FC	103

26 Jacques Copeau as the Magician in *L'Illusion*. DC   106
27 Suzanne Bing as Célestine, the sorceress, in *L'Illusion*. DC   107
28 André Barsacq's design for *Santa Uliva* in the cloister of Santa
    Croce. FC   115
29 *Savanarola* in the Piazza della Signoria. FC   117
30 André Barsacq's design for *Le Miracle du Pain Doré* in the
    courtyard of the Hospice de Beaune. FC   119
31 A scene from *Le Miracle du Pain Doré*. FC   121

Illustrations accredited "FC" are from the Fonds Copeau at the Bibliothèque de l'Arsenal, Paris, and are reproduced by permission of the Bibliothèque Nationale. Drawings ascribed to DACS are copyright of the Design and Artists Copyright Society Limited. Other illustrations are from the Dasté Collection (DC) and are reproduced courtesy of Marie-Hélène Dasté.

Preface

Even the geniuses among theatre directors in the twentieth century have needed a genius. The art, if it is one, is in its nonage and trial and error still the most practised method of learning its crafts. If, like a Renaissance painter serving his apprenticeship in the workshop of a master, Jacques Copeau had been able to article himself, it would have been to the Director of the Moscow Art Theatre. His introduction to a French translation of Stanislavski's *My Life in Art* concludes:

Dear Constantin Stanislavski, I have never had anyone to guide me in my art. I have never known that living, familiar yet formidable presence, which is both harsh on us and considerate, which every day, through the gift it makes to us of itself, seems to have the right to demand the best from us.

But among those whose words I have found instructive, whose example has sustained me, it is you, dear Constantin Stanislavski, who I would like to have called my master. Perhaps you would reject such a title, you who have written: "I know that I know nothing . . ." Then, I tell you I like you for your modesty, your nobility and your intrepidity.

In my own attempts at directing a rural community theatre company I have, without realising it, been sustained by Copeau. I mention this, not through immodesty, but to communicate a sense of recognition that I have felt in researching this monograph, the constant revelation there has been that the lingua franca of a certain kind of theatre and drama work in England and America today has its origin in work that was done by Copeau in Paris and Burgundy between 1913 and 1929. In France the debt to him is well known, and his influence has at times been almost oracular. His alumni, including Charles Dullin, Louis Jouvet and Etienne Decroux, have in turn become mentors to a third generation, including Jean Vilar, the director of the Théâtre Nationale Populaire, Jean-Louis Barrault and Marcel Marceau. In a fourth generation names have been perhaps less important than a searching for ensemble ways of working, of decentralising the cultural phemonenon of theatre and of restoring the arts of the entertainer to the portfolio of the actor.

Neither in England nor in America (with the exception of a couple of years at the end of the First World War) have we had Copeau's work to sustain us until recently. He himself never wrote a "Life in Art" and, although since 1974 his daughter Marie-Hélène and various collaborators have been publishing his papers as a series of *Registres*, this monumental labour of love is still only two-thirds complete at the time of writing and a full translation into English seems unlikely. There has been, however, a work-a-day transmission of useful intelligence between English-speaking professionals (and committed amateurs) that has had a substantial effect on the practice of our theatre. In drafting this preface I made a list of some of the techniques and areas of work where I now realise Copeau's initiatives to have been crucial to the development of twentieth-century drama. In no particular order: drama games; improvisation; animal mimicry; ensemble playing; writers-in-residence; *commedia dell'arte* revival; mime; mask-work; repertoire rather than repertory; community theatre; theatre as communion . . . and so on.

As I write I realise that to dwell on each topic here would be to make a meal of the hors d'œvres, and anyway Copeau's work should be seen in its integrity, not as a list of separable items. But there is one of his preoccupations that can best be appreciated now: the continual search for appropriate means of renewing the relationship between training and performance, of practising for one's practice. Many actors consider they are trained because they have had some training; this is not an attitude much to be found among musicians, but then it is relatively obvious how to practise objectively when you are not yourself your own instrument. Yet even singers take a much more practical attitude to their own voices (as do dancers to their bodies) than most actors to their means of expression. The very plurality of those means is often held to be the problem. But there is also (and a mis-reading of Stanislavski may have much to do with this) a prevalent notion that, in order to improve, all one really needs as an actor is more and better parts to play. Copeau wanted his actors to improve *for* their parts, not through them, and that improvement he saw as being of the whole person, not just an individual's technique. He was concerned, also, not to develop the actor solely in isolation, but as part of a *confrérie*, a brotherhood or community of performers who would learn and grow together and whose performances would be a collective expression of their sense of that growth.

Such a relationship between training and performance must stem from a different attitude to that of "go to drama school, then get a job if I can" which underlies current practice. The survival of the fittest, which is supposed to be the virtue of this system, can all too often mean the survival of the most cynically determined. How, then, have some English actors (and directors and teachers) gained access to the alternatives which Copeau proposed? I mentioned that little has been published in English about Copeau's methods until recently. In his foreword to Michel Saint-Denis' posthumous *Training for the Theatre* (edited by Suria Saint-Denis and published in 1982) Peter Hall writes that "my own personal debt to Michel is enormous. In 1961, at my request, he joined the directors of the Royal Shakespeare Company . . . He gave me ballast and direction when it was critically needed . . . He was a superb teacher who loved the young. For him the young were instinctive and giving: he took from them as much as he gave. They were also dogmatic and obstinate; but not for long with Michel. And theory was always subjected to his sceptical (and very Gallic!) challenge. He believed, of course, in craft, in technique, but only as a *means*. Acting was not a trick to be learned and then performed; it was not an imitation, but rather revelation of the whole human personality . . ."

Saint-Denis was Copeau's nephew. As a boy, he says, he played truant to go and see his uncle rehearse during the day and then, in the evening, he would go back to the theatre to see him act. After the First World War he became his apprentice, collaborator and, ultimately, successor. Saint-Denis in turn has had a profound influence on the ideology and working methods not only of the Royal Shakespeare Company, but also of the Old Vic and the Royal Court. During his years in England (where he exiled himself after the dissolution of the Compagnie des Quinze, the troupe that he directed as successor to Les Copiaus) he revised and developed his uncle's ideas (as Copeau would have wished, since he too was against dogma) but never ceased to acknowledge their source. He also founded two schools, the London Theatre Studio before the Second World War and the Old Vic School after it: it is largely through the alumni of these that the practical intelligence of which I spoke earlier has been handed on. Influential as those institutions have been, they have, however, proved impermanent. Saint-Denis' subsequent transatlantic plantings, the National Theatre School of Canada and the Juillard School Drama Division of the Lincoln Centre Project, New York, seem hardier.

But Saint-Denis has left us no disciple in his turn, and ideas such as Copeau's (which are nothing if not passionate) cannot be kept healthy by institutional means alone. It is as an aid to their future propagation and, for readers and theatre workers outside France, towards a proper understanding of their origins, that this book has been written.

Acknowledgements

Since Copeau's writings are little known to English readers I have quoted more extensively from his French publications than might otherwise have been the case. All translations are my own, unless otherwise stated. Access to some of Copeau's out-of-print writings has been considerably eased by republication in volumes I–IV of his posthumous *Registres* which have been prepared under the dedicated and beneficent supervision of his daughter, Marie-Hélène Dasté. Two further volumes are in preparation. Madame Dasté was kind enough to let me have an advance copy of *Registres IV* which contains a wealth of hitherto unavailable material on Copeau's work in America. She also painstakingly went through the draft of this book and many improvements in substance and correction of detail have been made as a result. I would also like to thank her for inviting me to stay "en famille" at Copeau's house in Pernand-Vergelesses: it is not so much the preservation of the house itself which makes a testament to her father's work, as the quality of life which it still sustains. From a few days there I learned more of the spirit which informed Copeau's later work than I could have gleaned from months spent in a library. There, too, I was grateful to be able to meet one of Madame Dasté's collaborators, Professor Norman Paul of the City University of New York. His *Bibliographie – Jacques Copeau* (published by the University of Dijon) has saved many hours of detective work and I thank him for his advice and scholarship.

Since 1963 Copeau's personal archives have been housed at the Bibliothèque de l'Arsenal in Paris and I am grateful to Mademoiselle Marie François Christout of the Départment des Arts du Spectacle for her assistance, particularly in obtaining illustrations. The busy teaching programme of a small department would have made it very difficult for me to undertake this book if the University of Exeter had not granted me a year's leave on half salary, but it was my colleagues who really made it possible by covering for me in my absence.

Finally, thanks to Jeffrey for keeping open house in Paris while I did the research, and to Penny and Rex and Takis Litsas for the summer house in which the first draft was written.

J.R.

1 Dramatic renovation

Theatre is not an elemental substance: the interaction between it and the other performing and fine arts makes it often hard to distinguish. The notion of a separable identity for theatre is often disregarded in the pursuit of new modes of human expression. The Greeks, for example, needed two Muses to inspire their drama, who in turn drew extensively on the resources of their sisters, Calliope and Terpsichore. Today these former virgins are known to have proved accommodating, but faithless: in our century alone, the list of those who have bought them new clothes would tax a Polonius. Jacques Copeau (1879–1949), working as a theatre critic in Paris in the early years of this century, became convinced that dramatic art had reached its nadir and that the time had come for new practical research into the European dramatic heritage; research which, rather than creating new forms in the first instance, would begin by re-discovering a true sense of form. Revealed from under layers of accumulated décor and greasepaint, he believed that the nakedness of his chosen medium would once again be seen to proclaim its virtue.

This research was to be singular in its purpose. Although Copeau's career divides neatly into episodes, his thinking did not; he was to shift his laboratory once because he had to and once because he wanted to, but the experiments which took place in it were always directed to the same ends. Thus, in order to be able to concentrate later on ends rather than means, it may be helpful at the outset to give a summary of those episodes, the first of which might be called "literary beginnings". Apart from a short period (1903–4) managing his family's business,[1] Copeau's work as a young man was all of a literary nature. After collaborating on a number of Parisian journals he succeeded Léon Blum as dramatic critic of *La Grande Revue* in 1907. The following year he co-founded the *Nouvelle Revue Française* (commonly abbreviated as the *NRF*) with Jean Schlumberger and André Ruyter. He directed its publications until 1913 when, at the age of thirty-four, he founded a new theatre, the Théâtre du Vieux-Colombier.

Although this beginning to a new episode in his career was deliberately adventurous, Copeau had previously been active as a playwright and, in particular, had gained some practical experience from collaborating in the staging of his own adaptation of *The Brothers Karamazov*. This first Vieux-Colombier company made a principled but hesitant start which culminated in the enormous success of Copeau's production of *Twelfth Night* (*La Nuit des Rois*), which joined the repertoire at the very end of the season. Then the outbreak of the First World War closed the theatre and the company dispersed. Invalided from the army in 1915, Copeau was able to spend most of his time preparing for the re-opening of the Vieux-Colombier. He read much, corresponded fervently with leading members of his company who were at the front and, most significantly, visited Edward Gordon Craig in Italy and Adolphe Appia in Switzerland to compare their thinking about the future of dramatic art with his own.

The third episode, the re-birth of the Vieux-Colombier, came sooner than he expected, and in a different country. Through, it is believed, the influence of Clemenceau himself (who had been an admiring patron of the Vieux-Colombier's first season), Copeau was able to take a company to New York in 1917 to carry the standard of French culture to a New World, which was still uncertain as to its obligations to the old one. There they mounted two seasons of work (Copeau also giving many lectures which were to prove seminal in the development of indigenous post-war American theatre), before returning to Paris in 1919 to re-establish themselves at their original theatre.

Thus began a fourth episode, a period of consolidation (1920–4) during which the Vieux-Colombier experiment came to be recognised as among the most significant of its time. Copeau, however, regarded its success as partial, disliked the effect that constant seasonal repetition of his concepts was having on his perception of them and decided that future development would have to stem from the Vieux-Colombier School (which he had founded alongside the re-established theatre), not from the company itself. Freeing himself from the commercial necessities of filling a theatre, he attempted to transfer the school to a rural environment, away from the superficialities of Parisian life.

This fifth episode started with disaster (the closing of the school through lack of funds), but developed into the founding of Les Copiaus, based in the Burgundian village of Pernand-Vergelesses. This new company included former members of the school as well as some of the Vieux-Colombier company who had followed Copeau to the country. For five years (1924–9) they created unique pieces under Copeau's supervision, plays which reflected the life and values of the rural community into which they became accepted and which also embodied their own sense of development as a troupe and as an acting co-fraternity. But again, as with the closure of the Vieux-Colombier, the undercurrent of Copeau's thought was stronger than the actual achievements on the surface of the stage and, having suggested that they reform under a new name, with a new director and a new writer, he finally dissociated himself from the troupe which bore his name.

The final episode (from 1929 until his death in 1949) does not lend itself to resumé. To an extent Copeau returned to his original vocation as a man of letters, still working occasionally as a professional director, but without a permanent company or school to give sustained expression to his ideas. In some ways his religious conviction now seemed to calm his dramatic fervour, though he still wrote passionately, for example, about the need to establish a truly popular theatre.[2] He was also in ill health, and to what extent this contributed to his increasing need for retreat from theatre practice and the world which it reflects will never be known.

We can now return to the beginning of this episodic summary and start to develop its themes. Here is Copeau's own recollection of his despair of the pre-war Parisian dramatic scene:

When I came to the theatre for the first time, it was as a critic, because I deeply felt that there was one thing which was perhaps the worst thing that was done in connection with the theatre, worse than the work of the theatrical people – that kind of leniency, that kind of facility with which the public and the critics accepted it, and I started to tell the truth about the theatre. I wrote in magazines[3] for about ten years what I thought was the truth about the theatre, and I was bold enough to say that not one writer in the theatre was really a man of the theatre.[4]

During this time he was careful not to become involved in the theatrical world, avoiding, for example, the dress rehearsals which it was customary for critics of the time to attend. His advice to young colleagues some years later was to go to the theatre with the public, not to "risk premature engagement of your judgements".[5] He liked to sense whether the audience were resistant to a production or let themselves be drawn into it: analysing their reasons was always instructive, sometimes illuminating. Sometimes, too, it would be necessary to visit a production several times before reviewing it: "you owe it to the author, you owe it to the interpreters, you owe it to your readers". Also, he might have added, he owed it to himself, for what he was doing during this time, whether consciously or not, was serving a kind of imaginative apprenticeship in the art of directing, raising his own ability to discern what was and what was not authentic to a playwright's intentions. The problem was that few, if any, contemporary writers seemed to merit such attention. In retrospect he wondered whether he was not excessively judgemental about the likes of Henri Bataille, but his sentences were not punitive. An American contemporary wrote:

In all of modern dramatic criticism I know of no work more salient, more honest and irresistible, than these papers which Copeau flung against the contemporary Parisian theatre. One thinks at once of the early fulminations of Bernard Shaw . . . To most critics the technique of destruction is a sweet thing in itself . . . The point about the essays of Jacques Copeau is their strange lack of this satisfaction in attack. They are not clever. They ring with a sobriety that is almost ponderous. They have the sonority of many numbers. They bespeak, indeed, not alone the indignation of one man, but of a generation: not alone in its passion to destroy and cleanse, but in its dream to create.[6]

That dream was to harden into an intention, then finally into an actual undertaking. In an essay which heralded the opening of his own theatre he finally went on the attack, decrying the "frenzied commercialism that (as it becomes daily more cynical) has debased the French stage". That essay, "On Dramatic Renovation", part diatribe, part manifesto, appeared in the *NRF* for September 1913. He wrote:

Most theatres have been snapped up by a handful of entertainers in the pay of unscrupulous impresarios; everywhere, most of all in those places where great traditions should safeguard some integrity, there is the same mountebank, speculative attitude, the same vulgarity; one finds fakery everywhere, excess and exhibitionism of all kinds, all the usual parasites of a dying art that no longer pretends to be otherwise; everywhere one finds flabbiness, mess, indiscipline, ignorance and stupidity, disdain for the creative and abhorrence of the beautiful;

what is produced is more and more extravagant and self-congratulatory, criticism is more and more fawning and public taste more and more misguided: that is what has roused our indignation.

Honest criticism had proved inefficacious: Copeau's indignation now swept along the Boulevards and up to and through the portals of the Comédie-Française itself. The French exponents of the "Little Theatre" movement were, to an extent, spared his lash: in particular André Antoine at the Théâtre Libre, and also some of the work of Lugné-Poë at the Théâtre de l'Œuvre, of Paul Fort at the Théâtre d'Art and of Jacques Rouché at the Théâtre des Arts. But even those directors Copeau now considered to be too sectarian in their interests; they had "unwittingly committed the folly of limiting their field of action to a narrow revolutionary programme". At the same time as the "Essay on Dramatic Renovation" was published, Copeau wrote to Antoine:

Your teaching has been the foundation on which my first aspirations and certainties have been laid . . . If one is looking for an example, yours is the only one that comes to mind . . . You remain, in our eyes, the sole living master.

But, he might have added, the master of one theatre only, not of *the* theatre. Antoine, who had at first sought to bring new foreign writers such as Björnson, Ibsen and Hauptmann before the French public, had, in Copeau's view, allowed their success to cloud his vision to the extent that he now allowed no style but naturalism on his stage, thereby denying it the essential theatricality of theatre. Also, he believed Antoine's use of actors to be just that: a directorial exploitation of what his actors could achieve without extension. As to the productions in other Little Theatres that were not of a naturalistic persuasion, he regretted that their directors had debased the word "art" to the point where it had become theatrically synonymous with "arty". Such theatre was reacting to itself, and not to life. A restoration of primary perception, such as had already taken place in fine art, was called for. In France, theatre was lagging behind the other arts in the search for forms appropriate to the new century. Elsewhere in Europe, Copeau stated, he was "familiar with the research . . . the projects and productions mounted by Meyerhold,[7] Stanislavski and Danchenko in Russia; by Max Reinhardt, Littman, Fuchs and Erler in Germany and by Gordon Craig and Granville Barker in England". Apart from one trip to London with his father, however, Copeau had no first-hand knowledge of the rest of European theatre, nor, for the time being, did he seek it. The new quest was to be made through action, not observation. He wanted to make conscious use of his indignation while it was still blazing: others too, he knew, had felt such indignation "and others before us have expressed it. But how many, even amongst the most fulsome, have slowly spent their anger! . . . We will have nothing to do with a discontent that does not find active expression."

That fervent tone in which he declared that something (or rather everything) was rotten in the state of French theatre sounds today like the call to arms of a young rebel. But Copeau was thirty-four when he wrote "An Essay on Dramatic Renovation" and what he was, so very emphatically, proposing was not a revolution. "We feel no need for a revolution. Our eyes are fixed on examples that are too great for that. We do not believe in the efficacy of formulas which are born and die every month in little artistic circles and whose boldness is mainly founded on ignorance. We proclaim nothing. But we have vowed to take action against everything that is despicable in contemporary theatre . . . we are preparing a place of refuge for future talent."[8] The present, then, could not simply be tweaked into shape by yet another *coup* (*de théâtre*, or otherwise). The critic turned activist could not raise an army to sweep away corruption – his oratory was that of the restorer, not the reformer – but he could set up one small, controlled experiment that, if successful, might provide an example for others to follow. But what right did a man of letters have to such a laboratory? Copeau believed that it was his very lack of previous practical experience and involvement that made him the ideal leader for such a quest. The hour had come for the banner to be raised by an angry *amateur*.[9]

In 1912 (when that hour had not yet come) a false start had been made to the experiment: Copeau wrote in his diary "*Artistic Direction* should not on any account be put in the hands of an actor. A professional man should be appointed director: someone who up to that point has had as little to do with the world of theatre as possible." As that "professional man" Copeau had two things to offer other than his sense of indignation: first his knowledge of plays as written, both past and present, and secondly his developed sense of dramatic intuition. Intuition, that is, in the sense that Henri Bergson, the contemporary philosopher, would have it: a sympathetic as opposed to a rational understanding. Bergson argued that, although the two principle modes of mental activity, instinct and intelligence, are sharply distinguished from one another, they exist together in symbiotic union. Their conjunctive operation, or intuitive faculty, said Bergson, was what informed all great art, and philosophy had neglected its study in favour of the rational, thus leading to distortions in our perception of reality. The outcome of Copeau's years of formulating critiques of the productions of others was not, therefore, to be the imposition of yet another intellectual theory. He had learned too much *savoir-faire* for that.

As well as a critic, Copeau was also an accomplished lecturer on theatre and a public reader of plays. His first solo readings were given in the Galerie Druet in 1911 and his inspirational manner of putting over a text kept him in demand throughout his career. His intuitive feel for what made good theatre was, he believed, to be found in his childhood experiences:

The windows of the house where I was born in the Faubourg St Denis, in Paris, opened on one side to low roof-tops, absolutely flat and uniformly grey. This surface offered vast scope to the imagination of a child such as I . . . It would have been totally featureless, like the dawn, the desert, or the stage floor after a performance, if there had not been, on the right, immediately next to the window on which I leant, a small, grimy, black building . . . Through a dirty window voices that were always angry reached me and, on some days, I could see in the gloom the naked arm of a woman, her hand lost in her hair, which she was plaiting. On the other side of the house, at the other end of my kingdom, was a deep, enclosed courtyard, cluttered with boxes and barrels. From morning till night a stooping man used to wrap and unwrap china, making a sharp, monotonous, clinking sound, amongst piles of straw and multi-coloured paper.[10]

The reminiscence continues with a description of how "the whole apartment was, for me, like a theatre". The lonely child filled every dark corner with the creatures of his imagination:

That is how we compose our first dramas, the ones we try out in our games, that we ponder over in our silences. That ineradicable childhood silence with its gloomy daydreams . . . is in reality the original crucible where our creative powers are forged, powers that we can only re-discover for the rest of our lives and then often only in a weakened form . . .

It is because of these games that filled my childhood . . . those mixtures of reality and poetry, because I wanted to re-discover and pursue them, that I came, belatedly, to the theatre and, perhaps, asked more from it than it can give. And it is, no doubt, so that nothing impure, nothing gross or brutish should attack those creatures of my imagination, that I wanted to take the machinery of theatre to pieces and re-assemble it, like a child does his toy . . .[11]

Children, though, do not often put toys back together again; that chore is usually left to the adults. The theatre was already in disarray when Copeau came to it and he knew that nothing short of the dedication of the rest of his adult life would make even a beginning to the work of re-assembly. Making the playhouse a fit place to release the world of play he saw as a spiritual, as well as a practical task, and not one which he would necessarily be able to finish:

Others, perhaps, will complete the structure. Let us at least try to form this one small nucleus from which action can radiate and around which the future can form . . .[12]

From Bergson, again, Copeau appreciated that conclusions were a function of intellect operating on its own, of Science, and that the interaction between life and Art could only be sustained by a philosophy of change. It was thus better to travel hopefully than to arrive . . . The playwright, Jules Romains, said of him that "out of a kind of messianic tendency, out of an inborn penchant to search in the future for his certainties and delights, he took pleasure in regarding his house as a provisional workshop, and all that he made there as a series of rough sketches, as feeble allusions to future work".[13] But in the quest for the Grail, it does not matter so much where you look, as how. Let's look, then, at how the first of Copeau's "provisional" workshops came to be set up.

For some time prior to 1913 his friends at the NRF had been gentling Copeau towards the notion of becoming a practitioner of what he preached. The first sign of his acceptance of such a new role came in 1911, with the production of his adaptation of The Brothers Karamazov at the Théâtre des Arts. He developed a working relationship as author with the young director Arsène Durec, and, when problems arose with the actor playing Ivan, Durec took over the part and left Copeau as "the only one in front of the stage". The production was a critical success (and would also have become a box-office one, if the Théâtre des Arts had not already been in irremediable financial difficulties). However, it gained a reprise a season later, and this time Copeau took sole charge of re-working the *mise en scène*. He had, in the meantime, resolved to set up a new theatre with Durec, or, possibly, even take over the Théâtre des Arts from Jacques Rouché. He charted the progress of their collaboration in a notebook:

I think that above all else a sound theatrical enterprise must defend itself against the charge of narcissism and the affectation of novelty. Our work should be sound, conscientious and well-intentioned, rather than original . . .

His thoughts on the directorship of the enterprise we have already noted; the theatre building, he wrote,

will be of very modest proportions; as convenient and well laid-out as possible, with no great luxury or excessive décor, a rather severe appearance.

Recruiting a company, there would be

No stars. Actors brought up through the work with complete discipline.

And, as regards staging, they were to "search for the simplest, most effective setting in terms of the play presented . . ." But, partly as a result of pressure from friends (particularly Schlumberger and Paul Desjardins, who saw Durec as an unworthy collaborator) and partly as a result of his own sense of the time not being ripe, Copeau broke up the partnership.

The search for backers and premises continued, however, and by 1913 his policies were fully developed and ready for publication. Every aspect of the new venture had now been thought through: they would set up away from the boulevards so as not to be thought, even, to be competing with the commercial houses; limited seating capacity would mean limited income, but the production style would ensure commensurately limited overheads; they would alternate productions during each week from a wide repertoire containing classics, revivals of contemporary successes and new plays; the company would consist of "young, unselfish, enthusiastic actors, whose ambition is to *serve* the art to which they are dedicating themselves". And, in envisioning production methods, he struck out at the devotees of the machine age who had recently found their champion in the playwright Henri Bataille:

We do not believe that in order to "represent the whole life of man" it is necessary to have a theatre "where sets can rise up from below and scene changes can be effected instantaneously", nor, ultimately, that the future of our art should be tied to "the question of mechanisation" . . . On the contrary! The restrictions of our stage and its crude resources will impose a discipline on us, by obliging us to concentrate true meaning in the emotions of our characters. For this new work all those tricks can be dispensed with: just leave us a bare stage.[14]

The bare stage of the childhood rooftops; but first it had to be found, leased and stripped. Like Artaud, his contemporary, Copeau has sometimes been admonished for lacking the practical bent necessary to bring about the full realisation of his ideas. Also, a myth persists that he was a man of independent means who could afford to sustain the losses involved in the pursuit of his vision. In fact, if anything was to distract Copeau from his purpose, it was the constant preoccupation with the necessity of balancing the books. Every prospective theatre was looked at with a businessman's eye: "I've just visited the Athénée St-Germain . . . I'm sending you a prospectus", he wrote to Schlumberger in January:

It seems to me just what we want, to start with. But we'll have to make our minds up quickly. The present director is leaving and if they haven't leased it by July, it's going to be knocked into flats. The rent would be 15,000 francs a year. There are 500 seats and I think boxes could be installed at the sides . . .

The implication of the mental income/expenditure arithmetic was obviously to doubt the viability of the present capacity. Schlumberger, furthermore, was depressed by the appearance of the place: "It's very shabby . . . the proscenium opening is very small. I prefer it to a theatre with ornamental plaster and caryatids, but the walls, ceiling and seats are in a wretched state." On another occasion he called it a "sordid alleyway". But they took it because it was in the right area: on the Left Bank, near the University, with good public transport to the rest of the city. The Athénée St-Germain was a little-known variety theatre situated in the rue du Vieux-Colombier (the Old Dovecote Street) between St-Sulpice and Carrefour de la Croix Rouge. So that a new clientele would know where it was, they called it simply the Theatre of the Old Dovecote (le Théâtre du Vieux-Colombier). A description of the alterations that were made, both then and later, will be given in chapter 4. For the moment we can concentrate on the new company, and Copeau's method of working it up. The actors were young, he was inexperienced and together they were going to mount a complex repertoire on a bare stage: the recipe would have to be perfect if the meal was not to be a disaster.

One of the few disagreements Copeau had had with Durec was over the casting of the crucial role of Smerdiakov, the epileptic valet and murderer. Copeau had his eye on an experienced actor, but Durec, to his lasting credit, stood out for a young actor who, he claimed, was made for the part. "At least you must see him," he said to Copeau, "then you can cast him or not." Years later, in a radio talk, Copeau recalled the scene:

Durec's office, a tiny cubby-hole which opened on to the staircase leading to the wings. The door half-opened and, on the threshold, appeared a sickly creature with an ambiguous smile and an anxious look. When I told him he was being considered for an important role in *Les Frères Karamazov*, he said simply: "If it's to play Smerdiakov, I think I can do it." He got the part and . . . Charles Dullin had his first great triumph. From that moment a great friendship sprang up. We paced back and forth, for hours at a time during the night, on the tarmac of the Boulevard des Batignolles, swapping ideas . . . And it was from these impassioned discussions that, sometime later, the first projects of the Vieux-Colombier were to emerge.

Dullin, with his circle of acquaintance among young actors, was instrumental in setting about raising the Vieux-Colombier company. When the time came (May 1913), it was his little studio flat that they used for auditions. Copeau sat down in the basement and made first observations on the candidates as they negotiated the vertical ladder that led down from street level.

There, in a rather grey light, the young men and women, for the most part hard up, and all unknown, from whom I was to make up a troupe of from ten to twelve actors, capable of peopling, despite their limited number, the entire world of comedy, drama and tragedy, filed in front of me. I didn't bring any very profound technical knowledge to their examination, but the intuition which has always been my chief guide. More than know-how and obvious talent, I was looking for a natural strength in each of them. More than the ease with which they could launch into a prepared piece, I let myself be influenced by the quality of a smile, by a surprise gesture out of role, by a statement that might be heart-felt. And I was lucky enough to find then, in one single audition, all those who, from that time on, formed a stable core, the living heart of the company.[15]

At the present time there is nothing unusual about the putting together of such a company of young enthusiasts, but for Copeau there were few precedents. An impression of the contractual expectations of the time can be gained from the following recollection: Copeau negotiated one actress, Suzanne Bing, down from a requested salary of 300 francs a week to 250. "Very well", she said, "providing I don't have to supply my own wardrobe." Copeau's agreement marks a significant moment in theatre history: the transition from the nineteenth century actor–manager buying in performances to that of an artistic director of a company intending to create productions. When that detail is multiplied through the range of activities involved in setting up a new theatre, one can begin to appreciate how innovatory the methods of the Vieux-Colombier were to be.

Rehearsals began on 1 July. The workmen were in the theatre, but Copeau did not want to rehearse there anyway; nor anywhere else in Paris, for that matter. His recipe was revealed to the public two months later in the "Essay on Dramatic Renovation": what was necessary was to create

an atmosphere around the actor that is appropriate to his development as a man and as an artist, cultivating his mind, inspiring his understanding and initiating him in the ethics of his profession. We will constantly bear in mind the development of individual talents as well as their subordination to the ensemble. We will fight against the incursion of tricks of the trade, against all professional malpractices and against the sclerosis of specialisation. In a word we will do our best to re-normalise these men and women whose vocation involves them in the simulation of every human emotion and gesture. As much as we can we will take them out of the theatre and into contact with nature and with life!

And so, at the end of June, they assembled in the village of Limon on one of the "beautiful hills which overlook the valley of the Marne". There Copeau had a house where he had been based with his family since 1911, a retreat where, for example, he had prepared with Jean Croué the adaptation of *The Brothers Karamazov*. The actors were found lodgings in the village, and their new life began.

For many it would seem, in retrospect, a time transfixed by its own special quality, like a slow-motion flash-back. Two newly-weds, Blanche Albane and Georges Duhamel, stayed with a farm labourer in the village:

Our room overlooked a rustic yard, itself opening on to the gardens. We left our window open all night. Characters from Shakespeare, Claudel, Molière or de Musset lamented, laughed or quarrelled in our dreams. Mingled with their cries came the sounds of animals and the calls of nocturnal birds, the scented breath of that happy hillside.[16]

Copeau, too, was unable to recall this time without lyricism:

I have lived in a little far-away village with my troupe. A big garden with high walls was our pleasant working place. For five hours every day we studied together the plays in our repertory. Two hours were given to first readings of new plays, which is a fine exercise for the intellect, as well as for vocal articulation. Every bush in our garden has been supposed to be all sorts of stage implements. Seated under the shadow of a tree we have discussed freely, each one speaking his mind.[17]

But the timetable was strict, and there were fines for being late. A further hour each day was spent on physical training – swimming, fencing or what were described as "rhythmical exercises" which everyone had to join in, even Copeau, since he was proposing to act himself. Not only did they read the plays in the repertory, but also other pieces and fragments of classical prose. And in the evenings, after supper, they improvised. Improvisation as a technique of preparation is accepted as useful by most actors and directors today – but again there were for Copeau no living traditions on which to base his explorations. He tried giving the actors some improvisations based on the characters and situations of whatever play they had been reading aloud during the day. Afterwards they sat around a table and Copeau would refer them back to the text, pointing up for them what was useful and discarding the irrelevant in what they had just done. Only at a later stage of preparation were they allowed to set the details of their performances, retaining, where relevant, the discoveries made in those early improvisations.

The advantages of the retreat to Limon were, therefore, more constructive than a mere removal from the distractions of Paris, and they were able to attract journalists who would make sure that their prospective audience in Paris understood that they were so: a certain "M.M.", reporting for *La Nation*, wrote:

Thus, while the repertoire widens, the fellowship of the actors deepens and the co-operative power of the group is intensified. Outdoor life sets the stamp of truth on their work; theatricalisms which spring to life behind the footlights wither in the sunshine. Here is no coaching for a performance, but the growth of a vital thing.

The very tone of these reports and reminiscences betrays – and why not? – an

1   Copeau and his first Vieux-Colombier company reading in the garden at Limon.
Seated, left, Charles Dullin; at table, Jacques Copeau; standing, two from right, Louis
Jouvet.

element of conscious myth-making. Things in the garden were, indeed, put to imaginative use as stage implements. However, the company's own horticulture was not as well tended nor the actors as creatively employed as might appear in the sunshine of reminiscence. Among such an *ad hoc* group there were, inevitably, unevennesses of temperament, ability and even loyalty to Copeau and to the values of the work. Copeau himself quickly realised that there were limitations to what could be achieved by those people, in that place and at that time, and began, as usual, to project into the future perfect: "They're still pretty bad", he wrote in a letter to a friend,[18] "I'll need at least two or three years to get a decent company together. But I will have one, one day . . ."

But while Copeau was already looking ahead, Dullin was more concerned with present achievement, or rather lack of it. He went so far, one Sunday morning, as to *write* to his director. Why write to a friend with whom he was supposedly in daily communication? Could the "impassioned discussions" they had had on tarmac not continue on grass? At all costs, Dullin said, he did not want the rest of the company to

2   Rehearsal of Molier's *L'Avare* at Limon, summer 1913. Left to right: Antoine Cariffa, Georges Roche, Louis Jouvet (seated).

assume that he was attempting to undermine Copeau's status. Nor did he want Copeau to think that. His complaint was couched very much in tones that implied "if I wasn't your friend and didn't believe in you and in what we are doing I wouldn't be telling you this". The gist of his letter was that the method of working was not providing the desired results. "You are encouraging a kind of acting that is in complete disagreement with what you have so often said", Dullin wrote:

> I've often seen you be hard, too hard, on some actors and now here you are, the director, and you're following the same line . . . you're encouraging their way of acting. Yes, since you don't say anything to them and, when you are acting yourself . . . don't seem to want to bring *life* to your characters, but often continue with the same tone as in your readings. Is that what you want? Is it me that's wrong, or is it you that, in *listening to actors*, are allowing yourself to be seduced *by the text*, and in your mind are making up for the shortcomings of their interpretation — and therefore not drawing out a full performance.

In effect the younger man, who knew some of his craft, was telling the older one, who as yet did not, that it was not enough to read, to analyse and improvise and then leave it to the individual actor to achieve a synthesis of the verbal and the physical, to find a means of embodying what had so far been an intellectual process. What Dullin was demanding was the kind of directorial contribution to the interpretative process that Copeau did not yet have the vocabulary to give. Indeed, the early productions of the 1913/14 season were not to be particularly distinguished for either their direction or their acting. As to their style, Antoine, for one, found it too literary, too much like a dramatised reading — the very effect that Dullin had found it necessary to discuss in his letter.

The exceptional quality of the productions, which possibly could not have been gained in any other way than through the retreat at Limon, was the sincerity and authority with which texts of the plays in the repertoire were rendered and the collective support that members of the company gave to each other while doing so. To have remained in Paris would have been to have kept the aspirations of the actors as individuals to the fore. Since they would not have shared life together, argued Copeau, they could not in honesty have shared its mirror, the stage. His evidence against the criticisms of Dullin and Antoine was that the actor *should* be able to take more creative responsibility. But the only way to obtain such actors would be to train them, preferably *ab initio*. The time in Limon was for him as much a sketch for what that training might consist of, as it was a preparation for a single season of productions.

For Copeau the director's art was relative, not absolute: since, unlike Craig, he refused to abandon actors to their inadequacies, he had to learn to work with them. If, in this first season, he sometimes fell short in practice of the principles which he had propounded it was not through lack of application: his work-rate was as prodigious as his ideas were abundant. Roger Martin du Gard describes his first encounter with his life-long friend and correspondent during the day of the first night of *Une Femme*

Tuée par la Douceur (*A Woman Killed with Kindness*), the opening production of the first season at the Vieux-Colombier:

Under the remains of a scaffold which was being hastily dismantled, in the dust from plastering, amid the tapping hammers, his torso moulded in a spinach-green sweater, his jaw-line buried beneath a fluffy scotch wool scarf, topped off with a soft hat with a wide brim . . . Copeau went at it like a demon. Extraordinarily agile, he leaped carelessly from the auditorium on to the stage, and from the stage into the auditorium. I could distinguish a feverish mask under the shade of the hat. He was re-arranging the blocking of the last act of the play, with the exactitude of a ballet-master, often stepping right to the back of the theatre to assess the total effect, he re-worked ten times over the slow assembling of the actors round the four-poster bed where the heroine is dying. "That's Blanche Albane," Gallimard whispered to me, "the wife of Georges Duhamel." Then he pointed out a great, raw-boned devil, to whom Copeau had just shouted "Don't move! You are crying. Don't gesture!" One could only see the figurant's back. He was standing at the foot of the bed, immobile, head down, shoulders heaving, seized up in a stance which expressed in a striking manner the grief of the valet in front of his expiring mistress. "That one," said Gallimard, "is our stage manager: Copeau's right-hand man, his name's Jouvet."[19]

The impact of Copeau's enthusiasm on Martin du Gard was such that, after a brief conversation over a ham sandwich in the stalls, the latter found himself, a few hours later, in charge of issuing cloakroom tickets to the first night audience. Another vivid portrait of the supercharged Copeau putting the finishing touches to a production comes from the playwright, Jules Romains:

The text has been learned a long time ago, the *mise en scène* fixed down to the smallest detail. All that remains is to try out the ensemble effect, to look at the linking of scenes, of acts which have been studied for a year in a somewhat haphazard order. All that remains is to scrutinise the costumes, the props, the settings, both in their own right and in relation to the rest of the production. Lights must be plotted, so too the length of scene changes and of intervals. Except for the text which is sacred (an admirable privilege, a hierarchy full of virtues, a prejudice, if you like, but a thrice blessed one . . .), except for the text, everything can be questioned again. Sitting in the first shadows of the auditorium, Copeau, feverish yet calm, examines his production, turns it round from every point of view, shakes it as if it were in a test-tube, looks for spots of impurity, areas of false transparency. All his mental energies are fixed on the present moment, but not absorbed, not overcome by it. However urgent the circumstances, however much was demanded by the flurry and bustle of these last moments, he remained in command of them.[20]

Copeau could not, and would not, work on a production without becoming involved in every aspect of it: set, props, lights and so on, and with costume in particular. His daughter Marie-Hélène says that it was he who taught her to make costumes.[21] He insisted on being called to every fitting, not because he wished to be consulted over every decision, but because he wanted to know about every detail, to have been involved in its progress personally, so that when the time came to put the puzzle together, he would be working with familiar ingredients. Some directors fade around the time of dress rehearsals and first nights; Copeau as the above accounts show, seemed to re-double his energy. He had no sense of it being a time for "leaving it to the actors, now": the pitch of the production had to be perfect, and for that it was necessary to keep on fine-tuning right up to the last moment. When such methods fail, they result in a kind of spurious febrility; when they succeed, as they did, for example, with *La Nuit des Rois*, every note of the production finally rings true to the score of the text. Years later one of those involved wrote:

I will never forget the first night of that wonderful run. Everything was already there: music, colour, warmth, exquisite finesse, both in terms of tenderness and of joy. For myself, for the audience as much as for the actors, we were afforded some of those rare moments when mind and soul have one accord; and as if touched by a kind of grace we felt ourselves transported by one single flap of a wing towards the eternal peaks.[22]

As in the descriptions of the work in the garden at Limon, a lyricism creeps into Villard-Gilles' reminiscence, as if working in the theatre was never more fulfilling than when Copeau's powers were vernal. Villard-Gilles attributes the spirit in the company directly to the attitude to work of *le Patron*:

What was marvellous about these first years was the friendly and trusting atmosphere which prevailed in the place. Copeau, demanding in work, intransigent over theory, showed himself to be always alert, paternal and good-humoured. He did moan from time to time, when it was necessary, in order to re-impose discipline when it was slack; but these rages did not last, and when he saw other heads bowed by these sudden storms, he couldn't help laughing, laughter which reassured us, a witness of his affection.

In this sense he was truly *le Patron*: like the owner of a bar or restaurant he took responsibility for the atmosphere of the place, wanting to make sure that everyone, staff and clientele, had a good time. And in *La Nuit des Rois*, adapted from *Twelfth Night* by Theodore Lascaris, first performed on 19 May 1914, Copeau found the perfect vehicle for the creation of such a festive atmosphere. It was the last of the plays that they had prepared in Limon to join the repertoire and the groundwork laid there had had time to mature and develop through further stages of rehearsal at the Vieux-Colombier. The disadvantage was that the company was exhausted after months of continuous performing and rehearsing. Furthermore, the last-minute panics were just that: for example, the designer (the English artist Duncan Grant) was still chasing round after actors ten minutes before curtain-up, making final adjustments to costumes which they were already wearing. Copeau (Malvolio) and Louis Jouvet (Sir Andrew Aguecheek) had had no sleep for two nights because, in addition to their other responsibilities, they had been lighting the show. But sometimes a true inspiration shines through such exhaustion, is even sustained by it, since no energies can be spared for distractions from the central purpose. The production, almost literally, "took off":

Copeau had the most developed sense of dramatic trajectory. He had a wonderful ability to provide illumination for us, to make us understand the overall movement of a work, the sum of those separate movements which are called acts, scenes, fractions of scenes and separate lines, those thousands of vibrations which add up, multiply and finally become, as in a bird's wing . . . flight.[23]

Waldo Frank, writing from the spectator's rather than the actor's point of view, described its "dramatic trajectory":

This comedy of Shakespeare has little weight as a dramatic action. It has infinite vistas of poetic charm. Its chief virtues are its airiness, its free dimensions, its swift succeeding silhouettes of character and colours of mood. It was precisely these qualities that came forth in Copeau's handling . . . The characters wove a design of fantastic movement. It lifted and wafted in the foreground of the play. And in the background, from out of the shadows . . . roared the laughter of the tippling clowns . . .[24]

Images of flight occur in many people's reminiscences of the production:

The Vieux-Colombier's staging of *Twelfth Night* . . . "drew" curved lines; it was fluid, free, as if improvised. The comedians seemed to be inflated by air, or as if stuffed with straw – creatures of the imagination; they had neither the hair, hats, nor swords of ordinary historical reality, and their acting had a peculiar, floating lightness.[25]

In 1931, when Copeau returned to the Vieux-Colombier to give two lectures under the title *Souvenirs du Vieux-Colombier*,[26] he chose *La Nuit des Rois* to give an extended reconstruction of an actual performance. The upstage area represented a public room in Olivia's mansion, a rotunda with white walls, containing only essential furniture and two shrubs in green tubs. The rest of the action took place on the forestage, separated off by a pink curtain to indicate the palace of Orsino, and a yellow one for outdoor locales. It was here that the Duke of Illyria appeared as the violins began to play . . .

You know how it goes:

> *If music be the food of love, play on . . .*
> *That strain again! it had a dying fall . . .*
> *Enough; no more;*
> *'Tis not now so sweet as it was before . . .*
> *Away before me to sweet beds of flowers;*
> *Love thoughts lie rich when canopied with bowers.*

And, as the Duke, followed by his noblemen, slipped into the shadows on the left, from the right another, separately lit, form emerged, slender, veiled in pink, a palm-leaf fan in her hand: Viola . . . Thus, from the outset, the comedy found its cadence and began to weave its threads. Hardly has the serious, slightly melancholic, voice faded: "rich when canopied with bowers . . .", than a clear, ringing female voice, that of Suzanne [Bing], is raised, taking our minds elsewhere, with no hiatus:

> – *What country, friends, is this?*
> – *This is Illyria, lady.*

And, almost at once, Viola, guided by the sea captain who saved her from the wreck, will follow the path that the Duke followed, to the left . . . And then, at the end and at the climax of

3   Suzanne Bing as Olivia in *La Nuit des Rois*, sketched at dress rehearsal by Berthold Mahn. (Note the "palm-leaf fan".)

these two scenes which have simply extended the musical impression of the prelude, being themselves like two latticed bowers, only then does the curtain rise to reveal the total dimension of the setting, in full light, and with the action fully under way . . .

> — *What a plague means my niece to take the death of her brother thus? I am sure care's an enemy of life.*
> — *By my troth, Sir Toby, you must come in earlier o' nights; your cousin, my lady, takes great exception to your ill hours . . .*

The tone of the comedy is set there and then. Toby Belch, played by Romain Bouquet, is strapped into ten kilos of padding. "The metal of India", "the youngest wren of nine", Maria, is played by Jane Lory, the tiny feet, the tiny hands. And the one who appears backwards, retreating with his hand on the hilt of his sword, sleeves flapping, bandy legs in flame-red stockings, head crowned with an azure topper with two pink wings stitched on to it, is the knight Andrew Aguecheek, mister Jouvet in person . . .

> — *Sir Toby Belch! how now, Sir Toby Belch?*
> — *Sweet Sir Andrew . . .*

Jouvet has, perhaps, never put more piquant naïveté into a comic role, more delicacy or more poetry. I don't think the truculence of Bouquet has ever been deployed with more largesse. The name of the character has stayed with him since. Among ourselves, we call him Toby . . . With Lucien Weber or Robert Allard in the role of the clown, Feste, with Cariffa or Vitray in that of Fabian, what a delicious quartet of clowns they made, in the famous scene of the duel, in that of the drunks in the night, with Maria, Malvolio in his night-shirt, the hanging lanterns and the bacchic singing:

> *O mistress mine! Where are you roaming?*
> *O, stay and hear: your true love's coming . . .*

I would like to sing it to you, but I am no singer.

And the scene with the letter . . . Maria has everything organised to wreak vengeance on the puritan upstart Malvolio:

— I will drop in his way some obscure epistles of love; wherein by the colour of his beard, the shape of his leg, the manner of his gait, the expressure of his eye, forehead and complexion, he shall find himself most feelingly personated. I can write very like my lady, your niece . . .

As soon as he sees this letter, left where he must notice it on a path in the garden, Malvolio will believe the Countess Olivia to be in love with him. Toby, Andrew and Fabian lie in waiting. Enter Malvolio, played by Savry, who took over the role from me:

— 'Tis but fortune; all is fortune. Maria once told me she did affect me: and I have heard herself come thus near, that, should she fancy, it would be one of my complexion . . . What should I think on't?

And whilst the beast soliloquises and begins to puff himself up with the dream which is going to destroy him, the three partners in crime, in the middle-ground, are having a romp, pulling faces, cupping their ears, taking steps to be nearer, turning back, hiding, risking a glance, chancing a word, stifling a laugh . . .[27]

Copeau, standing on the very stage where the action first took place, went on to read most of the ensuing scene, indicating, no doubt, the actions and reactions of the characters, impersonating the original impersonators.

La Nuit des Rois was more successful, both in income and "estime" than any of the weary company had dared think possible. Towards the end they had rehearsed in whispers, their voices were so tired.[28] Then there was only time for fifteen performances before they had to leave for a tour, but these were enough to offset any impression of tentativeness the public might have discerned in their earlier efforts and to ensure that the company had a future in Paris when they returned. There were many "rave" reviews, notably by Henri Bordeaux, perhaps the most influential French critic of the time. He wrote in *La Revue Hebdomadaire*:

The actors of the Vieux-Colombier play this imbroglio marvellously well: M. Jacques Copeau gives the steward a melancholic face which draws catastrophes to it. M. Romain Bouquet makes Toby Belch into a resplendent drunkard, overflowing with joviality, and M. Louis Jouvet interprets the pitiful Aguecheek as an English clown, slow-paced, in yellow and white, with a pallid face, as if drained of colour by the light of the moon, and the voice of a frightened schoolboy. Mlle Suzanne Bing's Viola is wistful and earnest as one could wish, but her stature is a little small next to Mlle Blanche Albane (Olivia) who unfolds and extends herself, slender, elegant and decorous, like a female figure painted by Burne-Jones . . . The play begins with a sigh and finishes with a song. I took rare pleasure in *La Nuit des Rois*.

4   Louis Jouvet as Andrew Aguecheek in *La Nuit des Rois*. "An English clown, slow paced, in yellow and white, with a pallid face, as if drained of colour by the light of the moon, and the voice of a frightened schoolboy."

5 Drawing of Jouvet by Mahn. "I knew 'twas I, for many do call me a fool."
(*Twelfth Night*, Act 2, scene 5.)

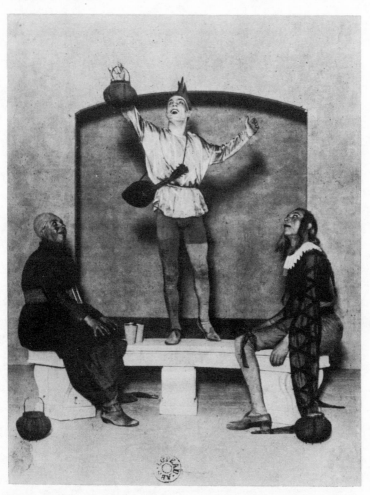

6 "Oh Mistress mine, where are you roaming?" Romain Bouquet as Sir Toby, Lucien Weber as Feste and Louis Jouvet as Sir Andrew. Note the lanterns, which were later to be used by the Copiaus.

7   Latér in the same scene (*Twelfth Night*, Act 2, scene 3):
    SIR TOBY He shall think by the letters that thou wilt drop that they have come
       from my niece and that she's in love with him.
    MARIA My purpose is indeed a horse of that colour.
    SIR ANDREW And your horse would now make him an ass.
(Mahn's drawing shows something of Copeau's facility for "natural" composition:
after the upward explosion of energy in the carousing, the conspirators now draw
inwards and downwards.)

Other critics realised that the standard format of praising or damning the actors one by one was to misrepresent the true success of the production: it charmed its audience by ensemble playing, not individual performances. Léon Daudet wrote, in *L'Action Française:*

Shakespeare is the most artful of chess-players. He has in mind certain combinations of heroism and sensuality through which he always moves his characters and which give his entire *œuvre* a sense of profound unity . . . at the Vieux-Colombier this cadence, sometimes quick, sometimes slowed down, has been respected, these hidden correspondences have been given their value.

The actors were playing for each other, for the audience and, above all, for the text. The result was that they, literally, found themselves in Illyria. Copeau himself was, understandably, in a state of contained joy. Roger Martin du Gard ascribed it to the fact that "in himself he had never doubted himself, nor the greatness of his mission, nor the final victory in the good fight to which he had given his all. He had in the highest degree, an awareness of being an *animateur* . . ."[29] Twenty years later, in his *Souvenirs* lectures, Copeau himself said:

Was I mistaken? It seemed to me that this was a moment of perfection. None of us were drunk with glory, nor corrupted by the life we led. So many forces were at work to divide us, to oppose us . . . It was a very brief moment, and so perfect a one, I say it again, that all who participated in it were fructified by it for the rest of their lives . . .

It was, he said, as if a sudden breath of wind had lifted their flight. For once the dramatic trajectory of the company coincided with that of the play they were presenting. Shortly afterwards, as Copeau laid plans for their second season (which was to have opened with a reprise of *La Nuit des Rois*), the hurricane of war scattered the flock. The actors had just signed two-year contracts. Copeau was to spend the next fifteen years looking for a wind that would once more favour him with shipwreck on the shore of Illyria.

2   The text

When I became a drama undergraduate (after receiving a literary sixth form education) a play, to me, was a play unless it had not been published, in which case it was still a script. In my first year I attended a seminar on "The sub-text", a term which was to become approved jargon in coffee-bar discussions. In retrospect it is obvious that that seminar intended more than mere refinement of student vocabulary: it was, rather, a remedial class in play reading. Our perceptions of a dramatist's intentions had previously been filtered through received literary critical values. The academic means of access to drama was, and (despite the emergence of theatre studies as an approved subject in schools) often still remains, to worry at the bones of a play as if it were a poem or a novel, rather than to receive the signals given by the playwright as to the intended *mise en scène*. Later, when rehearsing with a director rooted in the French tradition, I began to realise the usefulness of referring to "the text" when working practically from such signals. "Text" is now so current as theatre terminology that it has, in turn, lost some of its significance: properly understood, any play worth performing has a text which points to its on-stage rather than its on-page identity. If a performance is to be true to the author's intentions, this identity must be respected. "Text", even in English, suggests the authority of scripture rather than script, and is something that, as an actor or a director, one does not lightly "go against". Its use implies a fundamental regard for the score of the work in hand, and that the rehearsal process will be one of excavation rather than fabrication. To the French, "le texte" is redolent of the old *lycée* exercise called *explication de texte*, reading a passage out loud before giving a grammatical analysis followed by a literary commentary. We left Copeau giving a new version of this exercise to his actors in the garden at Limon. It was naturally the first exercise for actors that he had evolved, since for himself reading out loud had always been a personal skill which required constant practice and deliberate development. So, too, with listening, a skill at which actors can be notoriously lax . . .

Now let us approach the trees again to rediscover our novitiates clustered in small groups. One of them is reading the office for the day out loud: Rabelais – difficult to vocalise. A young woman is sewing attentively. Two young people are listening at the same time as fixing their gaze on the formations of trees on the horizon. Further away, two young women are sitting on a bench. One is reading Montaigne to the other, trying to render it as simply as if she were telling a story, but finding it difficult.[1]

It was not enough just to read to express the sense, however difficult. Copeau added a tonal objective. These daily *lectures à vue* were tasks set by him to increase the

24

troupe's ability to vocalise a text at sight, and, in turn, to hear and understand it. Implicit in this technique was a search for intellectual as well as vocal flexibility, a quickness of mind that could decide *while reading* on the "explication" of the author's intentions and give the text (including sub-text!) instantly appropriate phrasing, emphasis and tone. Another visitor to Limon wrote:

Copeau thinks, rightly, that this reading out loud is the perfect exercise for mouth and mind. There is a gentle rivalry which is the best proof of the difficulty of such tasks, and one is astonished to see actors, who for the most part have gained renown and favour from the Parisian public, buckling down to this kind of work.[2]

If the exercise was merely a technical one it would, presumably, have been more productive if the actors had read material to each other which was at least relevant to, if not part of, the repertoire which they were about to present. But in these, and later exercises, Copeau was concerned more with the education than the direction of his actors, wanting them to have as wide an individual and collective cultural field of reference as possible. In the end, he hoped, the kind of direction they would need as a result of this preparatory work would be quite different from the temporary expedients he was having to resort to in order to prepare for their first season at the Vieux-Colombier. Coherent background reading would, anyway, have been impractical, since that first repertoire declared its eclecticism in a way that defies any attempt to discern what a present-day repertory company would call an "artistic policy". Twenty-six plays were announced of which ultimately fourteen were produced, together with three that were not in the original list. Classical writers included Aeschylus, Euripides, Molière, Racine, Shakespeare, Heywood, de Musset and Merimée. Contemporary authors were Ibsen, Becque, Renard, Porto-Riche, Courteline, Wyrpianski and Shaw. The sole common denominator to this extensive (not to say daunting) list was that the contemporary dramatists had at least some title to the status of the classic writers as *poets*. By poet, Copeau meant a true descendant of the winners of the tripod at the Festival of Dionysus; writers who, whatever they wrote about, expressed spiritual and moral, as well as social, points of view.

In a lecture that he gave (in English) in Cleveland, Ohio in 1918, Copeau explained the basis of that first choice of repertoire:

I will tell you what we wanted to do. We wanted a place for the poet. We wanted a theatre for the dramatic works. We didn't want a theatre for *grands courturiers*. We didn't want a theatre for stars, or for anything else than poets . . . there was not only no theatre for the poet, but there was no poet . . . It was because the stage was something unclean.

That lecture, "To the Playhouse", is worthwhile reading[3] for the English-speaker, since the effort of communicating in a foreign tongue gives a more direct sense of Copeau's ideas than translations, which often retain the abstraction of the French, but lack its clarity. Some critics, notably Henri Bidou in *Les Lettres*,[4] found even Copeau's French too academic and idealised for a theatre practitioner. But a call to arms that does not seek to promote an ideal provokes little voluntary response:

we must first purify and honour [the theatre] by recalling to it the great works of the past so that the writers of today, regaining filial respect for a stage that has become tarnished, will want to do well on it in their turn.

Our first concern will be to establish a sense of veneration for the ancient and contemporary classics, both French and foreign. We will offer them as a constant example, as the antidote to bad taste and aesthetic fashion, as the standard for critical judgement and as a vigorous lesson for present-day playwrights and their interpreters. We will try to put ourselves in *a state of receptivity* when we encounter these works from other times which are all too often disfigured by the mechanical habits of certain actors and the routine of a supposed tradition!

What Copeau's manifesto for that first season, the "Essay on Dramatic Renovation", proposed was a period of dramatic convalescence for the restoration of the former powers of the medium, in order that new poets would want to use it in preference to, say, the novel or, as seemed increasingly more likely, the medium of film. In order to achieve this restoration the old masters could offer not only spiritual and moral values, but also a proper understanding of structure. They had rightfully been called poets, not only for what they had to say, but also for the form in which they said it and the ability to synthesise the two, to create a style which was popular in their own time yet transcendent of it. The Vieux-Colombier repertoire, in order to restore the medium for future use, was to centre on such exempla; plays whose matter was subsumed into their manner. The director's attention could thus focus on the re-discovery of structure, knowing that in doing so the truest possible service would be given to the text. The result would be to restore form to the actor–spectator relationship, a form which contemporary writers could then take up and make significant use of.

In the meantime, almost perhaps with some reluctance, new works were to be given their chance. The Vieux-Colombier enterprise had been proposed and fostered by the writers of the *NRF* and their immediate circle. Jean Schlumberger, for example, had become Copeau's commercial manager and had coped with all the bureaucracy involved in the alteration and installation at 21 Rue du Vieux Colombier, while Copeau was away in Limon with the company. Henri Ghéon organised a series of afternoon poetry readings in the theatre: all *NRF* members subscribed literally to its identity as a playhouse for poets. Naturally they too would expect access to its platform, and the proposed repertoire included new plays by some of them, as well as Vielé-Griffin, Claudel, Suarès, Arnoux and Copeau himself.

In order to understand why Copeau was writing for the theatre of which he was the director (and on whose stage he was frequently to appear as an actor), it is necessary to know something of his admiration for Molière:

A dramatic epoch is always characterised by the appearance of a great dramatic creator who holds in himself the solution to all existing problems. When Aeschylus was alive in the fourth century BC, when Molière was alive, there were no problems, no questions about theatre. There was a fertile presence making itself felt and from which everything else could flow; for one must not picture Aeschylus, for example, as a writer who fashions a play in his study and then gives it to an impresario to look at. The Greek theatre was Aeschylus, a man who was not content to merely write immortal verses, but also knew the declamation needed for his text, knew how to compose the music which would sustain that declamation, knew how to carry that style through to the actor's costume, his mask, his way of acting, knew, furthermore, how to supervise the architecture of a theatre. So when, by the same token, much nearer our own times, a Molière arrives, he takes, because he has so much in him, because he is the theatre made flesh, responsibility for all that and he transforms everything; he transforms comedy; he creates a comedic form; he creates a form of interpretation, and that is corroborated by the eye-witness accounts of his contemporaries, who said that Molière played comedy in a way that no one did before him and that no one has been able to re-create since.[5]

Copeau was fully aware that he was not the new Molière, but that was not going to stop him attempting everything that Molière attempted. Such a range of endeavour was vital to the attempt at dramatic renovation: Copeau felt he must take on board all the roles that Aeschylus and Molière had fulfilled in order to experience what they had experienced. Only then could he lead and direct his company's quest intuitively rather than academically.

Thus, although this chapter is primarily about Copeau the director working on a text, it is pertinent to follow first the story of his own attempts at being the provider of it. It was only as a result of those attempts that he was later able to say:

If I have brought anything to the theatre, if I have at least indicated what could be brought to it, it pleases me to think that it is . . . a releasing of the human spirit onto the stage by means of a profound and well-assimilated technique which has, as its consequence, the direct domination by the poet of the dramatic instrument.[6]

The first of his plays to reach the stage, *Brouillard du Matin*, was presented by the association of former pupils of his old school, the Lycée Condercet, at the Théâtre Réjane in 1897. Other early pieces were either not finished or not performed. In 1901 he began work on *La Maison Natale*: this was the play which was announced for the first Vieux-Colombier season. It was, in fact, nothing like ready. Although Copeau read the first act to André Gide in 1912, the second act was not finished until 1915. In the post-war seasons of the Vieux-Colombier it was again announced every year. It was finally finished and given by the company, as part of its last season, in December 1923. The failure of the production then was probably one of Copeau's main reasons (though, by his own admission, he was not thinking rationally at the time) for calling a halt to the Vieux-Colombier experiment. He wrote to his friend, the novelist Roger Martin du Gard: "Very poor box-office, *La Maison Natale* is a flop, flop, flop! But I'll put it behind me. Soon, I hope, I shall be born again. I shall grow young again."

The play was sunk by the critics who reported it as being "profoundly boring", "vaguely Ibsenesque" and "losing itself . . . in tirades that have nothing to do with the question".[7] When first conceived Ibsenism had been a virtue; now the play seems to have committed the worst sin possible in the most fashion-conscious of cities: it was out of date. But respected figures in the worlds of theatre and letters took a different view. Lugné-Poë, Antoine, Paul Fort and the philosopher Henri Bergson all found it a strong, remarkable play, even a masterpiece. Antonin Artaud wrote to Copeau:

you have written a work in which sublime events take place, one of the most beautiful works for the theatre of all time. I admire the way in which you have understood how to make your characters say *everything* that is relevant to the circumstances which constrain them; how each of your characters *empties* his *entire* heart and mind in front of us at precisely the moment we were hoping they would do just that. Your actors laughed last night at my enthusiasm. They were wrong. Your agonising play stirs up questions which are too fundamental, its events present us with a mass of beauty which is too overwhelming and too total, and above all too appropriate, for those that act it – it is you who have the right to smile at the felicitous effect which you produce.[8]

La Maison Natale is an introspective piece, evoking the dreaded figure of Copeau's father and the over-protective figure of his mother – the household tension that had created the childhood silence which we have already recalled. Such intense self-revelation appealed to Artaud, but it also brought accusations that, as a writer, Copeau was expressing a sensibility which was contrary to his supposed objectivity as a director. The keynote of the artistic eclecticism of his seasons had been disinterestedness, letting the theatre (and its poets) be its own policy. As director and actor Copeau had been passionately engaged, but not personally susceptible. As playwright he had become vulnerable in a different kind of way. Now he felt a need to be out of public view while his wounds healed.

His reading had been leading his thoughts back to the Dionysian festivals *before* the time of Aeschylus: the seasonal, choric expression of a community whose prosperity, both material and spiritual, still stemmed from the worship of, and exultation in, natural forces. The work which had been developed in the Vieux-Colombier School since 1920 could, Copeau believed, now begin to seek such roots. He moved it to Burgundy where, after an initial disappointment and a reduction in the scale of the enterprise, a new company/chorus was able to rehearse, as in 1913 in Limon, out of doors as much as possible. They lived in a village and shared the life of its inhabitants and thus ". . . learned to love this corner of France where we all sing: the old ones, the vine, the sky and man himself, when the wine moves his heart and releases his tongue".[9] Now for the first time they also performed outdoors, on a booth stage, at fairs and local festivals, or in a tent erected in a private field or garden. The spirit and natural energy of the country festivals (in which the actors both participated and then, at other times, were able to recreate through their own performances) was best expressed in works that resulted from the collective creation of the whole troupe. But Copeau, in his new role of dramaturg, found it necessary to provide much of the material, especially in the early years of the company's existence. A short play on a local theme, *Le Veuf*, was first performed in Demigny in May 1925; *Mirandoline* (after *La Locandiera* by Carlo Goldini) a week later; *Arlequin Magicien* (a comic *divertissement* in thirty scenes mixed with songs and dances, after an old Italian scenario with textual borrowings from Molière) was given in Meursault in August; *Les Cassis* (after *Las Olivas* by Lopé de Rueda – a short piece evoking by means of song, mime and words the cultivation and harvesting of blackcurrants, an important crop in Burgundy) entered the repertoire in October and *L'Illusion* (after Corneille's *L'Illusion Comique* and *La Celestine* by Fernando de Rojas) was first played in Basle in October 1926. This last was a full-length play, the first to be attempted by the new company. It featured a prologue, an induction and an epilogue spoken by Copeau himself in the role of the Actor. In the following year he adapted Ruzzante's *L'Anconitaine*, his last offering to the company.

The troupe, which had been called "Les Copiaus"[10] (The Little Copeaus – a name given to them by the local peasants) disbanded in 1929, to re-form under the leadership of Michel Saint-Denis and to become known as "La Compagnie des Quinze". Copeau's last gift to them was – a writer. Since 1926, as Copeau gradually withdrew from the work, more and more of the company's writing had been done by Saint-Denis in conjunction with another member, Jean Villard. But they, no more (and probably less) than Copeau could aspire to the role of "poet". All were aware that an established outside writer, if attached to them in sympathetic collaboration, would add a dimension to the company's work that they could not supply from within.

The Copiaus' log-book entry for 3 January 1929 reads:

Le Patron departs: he is to direct a play by André Obey in Paris.

Then, on 14 May:

André Obey . . . came from Paris to see *L'Illusion*. Full house, very successful, numerous curtain calls.

Copeau believed that it was a benevolent genius which had brought him there. He had known Obey for several years:

I was drawn to him by a fondness for his impressionable nature – he was restive and a little wild, very direct – and also through my confidence in his ability. In works which were at some remove from my personal taste, I discerned in him a rare gift: that of dramatic measure. He evinced his friendship for me. At a time when authors seemed to have forgotten me, theatreless director that I was, Obey went out of his way to make his regard for my work plain.[11]

The Comédie-Française was taking an interest in Obey's work and he was widely considered to be among the best of the new generation of writers in Paris. Yet, two years after that visit to Lyon to see the Copiaus in *L'Illusion*, his plays were being brought up to the capital like peasant produce to market. In 1931 the Compagnie des Quinze made a brief return to the Vieux-Colombier (which had been used mainly as a cinema since 1924) with two products of their association with Obey: *Noé* and *Le Viol de Lucrèce*. In a programme note these were described as

the first fruits of a close collaboration between a dramatist and a company of players. The collaboration was smooth and happy, but at first it required such an effort of adjustment that it would have been impossible for us to adapt ourselves to more than one author at a time.

Perhaps, then, although Copeau had written *for* them, he had not been sufficiently relaxed about his abilities as a writer to share the scripting process with them, in the rehearsal room. Obey, on the other hand, was eager to accept the challenge and fully realised that his own work would be metamorphosed as a result:

If he had never seen the work of Copeau's troupe he would presumably have continued to write plays, but they would certainly have been very different from the plays he wrote for the Compagnie des Quinze. It would have been pointless to have written a play such as *Le Viol de Lucrèce* for the ordinary theatre, because it demands actors equally highly trained in speech and mime – which the Compagnie des Quinze were able to provide. And yet, as Copeau so often pointed out, there was nothing novel in their technique. It was based on the two great traditions of French theatre – fine speaking and expressive miming.[12]

Marie-Hélène Dasté, one of the former pupils of the Vieux-Colombier School, says that, in fact, one of the things that their training had not given them was a technique of fine speaking: their skills were mainly corporeal and the long speeches which Obey wrote tended to be given to actors with a different training such as Suzanne Bing who played Boberiot in *Le Viol de Lucrèce*. Marie-Hélène Dasté herself played Lucrèce, but modestly describes her voice as *"mal placée"*.[13] And for *Noé* they bought in Pierre Fresnay to play the vocally demanding title role, although this was later taken over by Saint-Denis himself. The troupe's real capital was its choral and ensemble movement, mime and mask work. This was the strength of later collaborations with their poet-in-residence, particularly *Loire* (another regional celebratory piece) and *La Bataille de la Marne*, which grew out of an exercise at the Vieux-Colombier School:

We decided that we did not want to treat the subject as a series of anecdotes in a descriptive way; rather, we wanted to get to the roots of an event by a physical representation . . . Having decided on a tentative order of events, we improvised various scenes showing different aspects of everyday life in a village in peacetime. These scenes were done simultaneously. Suddenly the bells of the church began to toll an alarm, warning that war had been declared. The inhabitants assembled in the village square. The moment of separation had arrived: the men called to the front and the distressed women left behind in the village. This was followed by the exodus of the whole population fleeing in panic before the invading Germans. Scenes were improvised of men in combat, of life and work in the village, the anguish of the women left behind. Finally, the armistice, with its reunion of families and their realisation of death and loss. Through our improvisations ideas gradually came to life and the framework of the play became clear.

Obey made use of our previous experiments, in which we acted several scenes simultaneously. He evolved a mode of expression, a kind of "musical" composition which used some real words supplemented by a sort of invented mimed language we had experimented with in Burgundy, which we called "grummelotage", or "the music of meaning".[14]

Thus the especial virtue of the Obey–Compagnie des Quinze relationship was that, rather than simply writing good parts for actors based on their improvisations, Obey was able to write to the stylistic strengths of a permanent company that had already served its apprenticeship together under Copeau. He had been their master, but had only been able to be their poet as a kind of pedagogical illustration of the possibilities of the role. Now the pupils had grown up and were working with a poet of their own age, one that Copeau had recommended as a suitable collaborator in the creation of the "œuvre nouvelle" of which he dreamed. Obey was not the Aeschylus, the Molière or even the Lorca that Copeau felt would come when the medium had been fully restored, but a true poet, nonetheless.

In order to gain an overview of the consistency of his attitude towards the position of the writer in the theatre and of his own efforts to fulfil that role before finally favouring another, we have rather accelerated through the episodes of Copeau's career. Let's return now to watch him at work at the Vieux-Colombier as a director of an established text, whether classical or contemporary. In a summary of his ideal way of working (written for the *Encyclopédie Française* in 1935), he proposed the following phases in the director's work on the text:

He receives a script from a playwright . . . after his initial reading inanimate pages begin to come to life in his fingers . . . Later, after more methodical study, the director will deepen these various notions. But at his very first contact, a tiny universe, both spiritual and concrete, begins to take shape . . . What remains in the director's mind, and not only in his mind but within reach of his senses, so to speak, is a feeling of general rhythm – the breathing, as it were, of the work which is to emerge into life.[15]

The director should then, says Copeau, work out a detailed, speech-by-speech plan of the action as he envisages it on the stage. Then, at the beginning of rehearsals proper:

The director should first call his actors together around a table and not on stage: first, in order to read the play to them and impress on their minds its meaning and rhythm, secondly in order to have them read their parts. This phase will last as long as the director is capable of sustaining it and the actors are capable of enduring it. It enables the director to explain the author's intentions and his own, to nip in the bud any incipient misunderstandings, to dwell on the beauties of the script and the basic principles of its interpretation, and perhaps to correct certain mistakes in casting before the actors have entered into their roles . . .[16]

Everyone who speaks of working with Copeau agrees that it was at this stage in the production process that he had most to offer. He seems to have had an ability, akin to that of a surgeon in a teaching hospital, to open up the body of a play and show what made it function. His years as a critic had left him with a practiced skill in exposing the heart of a text and proposing how to deal with it. In the 1935 article he next suggests that the director should take his actors through the *mise en scène* that he has previously worked out. But this was not the way that he had himself always worked in practice. Here, for example, is a description of him at work during the 1917–19 seasons in New York:

Copeau's method . . . was to have the play read on stage, each actor sketching out in tone and movement his conception of the part, while Copeau would keep saying: "Go ahead: do something, do anything!" At a certain moment (sometimes it took days before this moment came), Copeau would withdraw, to return with a detailed *mise en scène*, complete down to the number of steps to be taken in any direction, in which he would have reinforced, developed and much improved each actor's idea of his part, and pulled them all together into a possible dramatic whole . . .[17]

Whether he started the process on the stage or off it, with the actor's ideas or with his own, the goal was the same: to envision a *mise en scène* (which one is, for once, tempted to translate literally as a putting-on the stage) that was of *of* the text, not *for* it, or derived from it. In the "Essay on Dramatic Renovation" he insisted that "all the originality in our interpretations . . . will come from a profound study of the text".[18] But the other half of the director's craft lies in the transmission of that study to the actor. Copeau learned this delicate business by trial and error: he came to it late, and had to be his own apprentice. We have read Dullin's criticism of the reticence of his first efforts when preparing the 1913 repertoire in Limon. Michel Saint-Denis says that at that time, Copeau told him, he had instinctively believed in the primacy of action in staging a play, but did not yet know how to develop it, since his own training had been in philosophy and literature. By the time Saint-Denis worked with him in the twenties, Copeau had acquired a personal vocabulary as a director that fully released his powers of textual analysis to the actor. Jean Villard-Gilles (who joined the company in 1920) recalls:

He excelled at this analysis. Think of the complexity of this art [of acting]. The actor has to do everything at once: play the character and the situation, speak and move, be part of the ensemble, throw his voice with enough force to be heard everywhere, and at the same time remain simple and natural. Copeau, out front, would guide him with sureness. He built him up to the co-ordination of all these mechanisms through internal workings.[19]

Saint-Denis expands on that picture of Copeau "out front":

His actors would rehearse *sotto voce*, without any eloquence, careful not to force the text, just sketching tempo and rhythm without trying to achieve anything too early. During rehearsals Copeau would move ceaselessly from the auditorium to the stage; if an actor was in difficulty he would talk to him freely but confidentially at the back of the stage. As an actor himself he instinctively knew when to grant freedom to an actor and when to apply the right kind of pressure during the successive stages of rehearsals.[20]

Let us now follow Copeau's own delineation of what those successive stages should be, and the actor–director relationship appropriate to each. We left him at a table with his cast, explicating a text for as long as he could sustain it and they could endure it. Before moving away from that table, Copeau continues, the director must have his production plan ready:

Since the play is essentially action, and an actor primarily a human being who acts, before going any further our director seeks to delineate the place, form and dimensions for this action.

For that he needs

a staging plan, on which he will locate, as accurately as possible without harming the flow of the action, the actors' places or positions as well as their entrances and exits.[21]

Then the action itself is to be organised, act by act, speech by speech, down to the slightest details. The director, says Copeau, should now devise the action he is going to propose to his actors in the minutest detail; their places, distances from one another, movements, relationship to set, furniture and props, pace of speeches, silences, tempi of exits and entrances. The first on-stage rehearsals (remembering that, with the repertoire system organised as he had it, there was no need for recourse to rehearsal rooms) would then be "devoted to the assignment of places": the actors would become familiar with the mechanics of the director's action plan, accepting or discussing his reasons for it. These discussions would give the director a last chance to revise the plan before sets (if any . . .) were built. Copeau insisted that this period of uncertainty should not be prolonged, since it might demoralise the actor.

So now the play is clarified, even though in summary fashion, from beginning to end . . . Actors and directors . . . know where they are going before they plunge into the actual interpretation. This work of interpretation becomes possible on the day that the actor . . . begins to speak his lines from memory and tries to harmonise what he says with what he does. At that moment even the most gifted actors seem to hesitate. There is a critical period during which the interpreter seems to have lost the feel of his initial grasp.

At this difficult stage the director should encourage the actor to identify physically with the character before attempting any emotional expression. This, says Copeau laconically, requires concentration and sincerity, but

here too the director is the actor's guide and mainstay. His task is not only to keep the actor in line and within the limits of his part, not only to indicate to him where he is near the truth, and not only to correct his mistakes, but also to understand the difficulties confronting the actor and to show him how to solve these difficulties. But it is by means of sympathetic understanding that he will exact his most active influence, provided that his experience with actors is long, objective and profound enough for him to know the specific sensitivity, temperament and ability of each one of them. It is dangerous to allow the actor too much freedom; but it is even more dangerous to stifle his spontaneity with blind coercion.

In this search for spontaneity both actor and director are vulnerable: the director in that he risks losing the actor's confidence if he is unable to provide the right keys to the right locks at the right time; the actor in that he is the one who has to be spontaneous, not once but many times over. The last thing he wants to feel, as he prepares the triggers to that spontaneity, is the director's manipulative hand upon him. It is for that reason, one supposes, that Copeau was at his most dictatorial in the early, outline stages of preparation. The later emphasis in rehearsals was on the actors' craft rather than his own. He quotes Granville Barker on this question for the director of finding the right balance between freedom and discipline for his actors:

The more he can leave the initiative to the actors the better. And when he cannot, let him emulate the diplomat rather than the drill-sergeant, hint and coax and flatter and cajole, do anything rather than give orders; let them if possible still be persuaded that the initiative is theirs not his. The Socratic method has its use, if there is any time to employ it; an actor may be argued out of one way of thinking into another. But the immediate effect of this may be depressing, even paralysing . . . the actor must then be heartened into starting afresh, and encouraged while he finds his way, and protected from the impatience of his fellow actors who have already found theirs.[22]

There is a cynical undertone to Granville Barker's advice: his director seems to need the poker-player's nose for how to make most profit from imperfect cards. Copeau preferred to believe in the perfectability of the actor, offering himself as mentor or *pater familias*. Whichever role directors cast themselves in (and there are many others – I have seen Peter Brook, for example, sit in on a discussion with his actors like a therapist facilitating a group session), it has to be one through which he can resolve the problem to which Granville Barker draws attention: the differing work rates of individual actors. It is not always the quickest who need the least attention – their speed may be the result of superficiality or of casting close to type. Arriving at a performance too soon, he or she may become bored or dissatisfied. To avoid that, the experienced director will provide obstacles, sometimes even artificial ones, along the way. On the other hand, an actor may be working too slowly, given the deadline and the state of the rest of the production. This may be because he or she is too secure (lazy) or too insecure (timorous). Either way, the director will not help by repeated demands to hurry up: pressing the pedal down further will not improve the carburation. Copeau's ideal director can focus on a variety of such actor problems and know where most of his attention should be given at any particular time. A sense of balance is required; he must provide a service without becoming servile. He must take the overview, get results from individuals that are right for the whole, but do so without being overtly manipulative and losing the actors' trust. Loss of such balance results in an uncertain working atmosphere which, ultimately, undermines the integrity of the performance.

But, despite his developed awareness of the need for careful planning of the stages of rehearsal, of transforming the poet's text into original action via the medium of the actor, Copeau was continually beset with difficulties in practising what he preached. In particular, the compromise to be struck (in a non-subsidised theatre) between available time and artistic objective was a constant source of dismay. When, in 1929, he gave up the production treadmill inherent in running a theatre and/or theatre company, he turned to the "profound study" in itself, publishing, for example, an edition of the complete works of Molière and, in collaboration with Suzanne Bing, translations of Shakespeare's tragedies and comedies. In the theatre of his mind, with the years of practising the possible behind him, perfect *mises en scène* could now be envisioned. Looking back, he did not allow himself many moments of actual attainment:

a few moments from *La Nuit des Rois*, from *Carosse* and from *Pacquebot*, though I will add a scene from the 1913 production of *L'Amour Médecin*, certain movements from *La Jalousie du Barbouillé*, at least three or four moments from *Conte d'Hiver*, two or three figures from *Fourberies de Scapin*, the assembly of the Ancients, the church scene and the entry of the young girls from *Cromedeyre*, this or that line from *La Surprise de l'Amour*, this or that tableau from *Le Misanthrope*, the last act of *Saül* . . . I don't think I'm being too greedy. I would let most of it go for scrap.[23]

When he said that, he was standing on the stage of the Vieux-Colombier giving a lecture prior to its re-opening for the 1931 Compagnie des Quinze season. Of all the obstacles he had faced as the director of that theatre – lack of time, shortage of money, inadequate resources – none had frustrated his vision more than the subject of the next chapter: the actors themselves.

3   The enemy of the theatre

Edward Gordon Craig's *The Art of the Theatre* appeared in 1911, some of it having been published previously in the periodical *The Mask* in 1908–9. Despite its patchwork format and Edwardian vocabulary, its impact can still be experienced today, as then, by anyone wishing to believe in the possibility of a theatrical renaissance. When Copeau stated, in his 1913 "Essay on Dramatic Renovation", that he was "familiar" with Craig's work, it was to those published writings that he was referring.[1] His immediate reaction to Craig's ideas would, one imagines, have been similar to that of Dr Alexander Hevesi (dramaturg of the State Theatre, Budapest) in his introduction to *The Art of the Theatre*:

I think Mr Craig is the truest revolutionist I have ever known, because he demands a return to the most ancient traditions of which we can dream. Revolution and revelation are not far each from the other, and he gives us both. His torch, destined to set on fire our pseudo-theatres, our monstrous and barbarous playhouses, has been kindled at the sacred fires of the most ancient arts. He discovered for us that in a rope-dancer there may be more theatrical art than in an up-to-date actor reciting from his memory . . .

Dr Hevesi then blames the Realists (as offering imitation instead of life) and the Machinists (tricks instead of marvels) for destroying the true Art of the Theatre. We have seen Copeau nodding at these sentiments, but he was perhaps not as inclined as Craig to spell art with a capital A: he did not see the theatre of the future becoming a single, pure medium that could flourish in isolation, like music, sculpture or painting. He would never join Craig in parting company with "the popular belief that the written play is of any deep and lasting value to the Art of the theatre", but he did agree that the ultimate blame for the decadence of their medium could only be laid at one door: that of the green room. He was fond of quoting Craig quoting Eleanora Duse:

To save the theatre, the Theatre must be destroyed, the actors and actresses must all die of the plague . . . They make art impossible.

During his years as a critic, Copeau had indeed found little to justify the use to which French actors were putting their predominance:

vain and arrogant, the latter are the true masters of the situation; their whims and their despotic ignorance rule the stage. A play is unrecognisable once it has passed through their hands. They modify the text, add, delete and transform it to suit themselves, they are supposed to be the collaborators of the authors and they are their tormentors.[2]

When he found himself in the author's seat (*Les Frères Karamazov*) instead of the critic's, there came one moment in rehearsal which gave perfect point to his complaint against the actor; early on he noted in his diary:

Today everything is going well. We have engaged Garry to play Ivan – not a dream Ivan, far from it, but a good, experienced actor much liked by the public.

But years later he recalled (in a radio talk) that his first impression soon altered:

Just as Dullin [who was playing Smerdiakov] was straightforward and modest at work, friendly in private life, poetic in his inspiration as a performer, so the actor who found himself entrusted with the role of Ivan Karamazov revealed himself to be pretentious, and, frankly, a cheapskate mountebank. We had just rehearsed the scene where Ivan discovers Smerdiakov hanging in his little room. We were going to carry on, when the actor in question took a few steps towards the footlights and addressed himself to me: "What I'd like", he said to me, "is to do something at that moment . . . you know . . . well, something like, for example, putting a candle out." The action, it should be noted, was taking place in broad daylight. I asked him if, for this important piece of stage business, he was intending to use a gun.

Shortly afterwards a dispute arose between Durec, the director, and M. Garry which resulted in the former taking over the part of Ivan and Copeau changing his seat in the auditorium once more.[3]

Copeau's word for M. Garry and those like him was "*cabotin*". Just as the theatre needed, he believed, to be de-commercialised, so the actors in it needed "de-cabotinising" – draining of false histrionics and the cult of the personality as a basis for performance. For Meyerhold, however, the *cabotin* was a figure to be admired:

The cabotin is a strolling player; the cabotin is a kinsman to the mime, the histrion and the juggler; the cabotin can work miracles with his technical mastery; the cabotin keeps alive the tradition of the true art of acting . . . In order to rescue the Russian theatre from its own desire to become the servant of literature, we must spare nothing to restore to the stage the cult of cabotinage in its broadest sense.[4]

Although there is, as Copeau was later astonished to discover, a remarkable similarity in their theatrical objectives, he could hardly have differed more from Meyerhold's use of the word "*cabotin*". For present purposes it is, therefore, best translated as "mountebank" or "ham" – a summation of those qualities that had already led Craig to abandon the actor as the true medium of dramatic art.

Thus Copeau, mentally at least, underlined certain passages in his copy of *The Art of the Theatre*: "The actor as he is today must ultimately disappear, and be merged into something else", for example. The question was, what should that something else be? Craig proposed the Übermarionette, but Copeau had seen the beginnings at least of a future based on the human frame in the performance of Dullin. The early war years of enforced practical idleness gave Copeau the opportunity of going to Florence to take up the issue with Craig himself. When he visited in the autumn of 1915, Craig's school at the Arena Goldoni was closed. But even if it had been active, Copeau would not have seen any actor-training there. Craig's conservatoire was for artists of the theatre according to his own definition, not for artistes. Designers, painters, mask-

and puppet-makers, even carpenters, electricians and printers, were to learn there an Art, not merely improve their craft. "For him", Copeau noted in his diary, "the actor is not an artist. One can do nothing artistic with the human face." Craig, of course, knew this to be a provocative lie. In *The Art of the Theatre* he had advised young actors to get hold of as many pictures of Henry Irving as possible and meditate on them "when losing hope that you will ever bring your nature as exhibited in your face and your person under sufficient command". And he showed Copeau Irving's make-up mirror, along with one that had been given to him by Tommaso Salvini.

He talks tirelessly in praise of Irving and Ellen Terry, his mother; and said, laughing, that he was a great fan of "the old acting". And he was even more lavish in praise of the Italians, Pettrolini, Novelli and especially Giovanni Grasso, the Sicilian.[5]

The visit to Florence helped Copeau to put his quest on a continental scale, to cease regarding his problem with the actor as a peculiarly Parisian one. Craig could proffer no off-the-peg solution to the paradox of loving acting but despairing of actors that was to plague Copeau throughout his career as a practitioner, but seeing the models and the maquettes in the various studios at the school reinforced his vision of the performer as part of a total plasticity, and reminded him of one possible line of enquiry already hinted at in *The Art of the Theatre*:

I should say that the face of Henry Irving was the connecting link between the spasmodic and ridiculous expression of the human face as used by the theatres of the last few centuries, and the mask which will be used in place of the human face in the near future.

But what kind of training would the body need in order to wear that mask? After leaving Craig, Copeau travelled to Geneva to meet Jacques Dalcroze and visit his school of eurythmics. Again, he had so far had access only to Dalcroze's written pronouncements. In notes towards the establishment of a school of his own, Copeau transcribed the following from a Dalcroze pamphlet:

It is the pupil who should teach the master, not the master the pupil. The role of the master should rather be to reveal to the pupil what he has taught him.

Here was an educational philosophy that could allow for the growth of actors as creators in their own right, providing an antithesis (and, hopefully, an antidote) to the only existing French acting school, that of the Conservatoire Nationale de la Musique et de l'Art Dramatique. In the early 1900s this school for the most part limited its objectives to teaching, by rote, the "traditional" method of playing one role in order to prepare a student for the *concours* at which actors were selected for the Comédie-Française.

Copeau had been present at eurythmic sessions at the Club de Gymnastique Rhythmique on the rue Vaugirard in Paris, but this visit to Dalcroze's newly opened institute was to provide a truer insight into his method. After the first session that Copeau observed, he noted "nothing in common with what I saw in Paris". What he

did see provided immediate confirmation of his own instinctive inclinations towards
the possibilities of actor-training, a perception that Craig had been unable to share
with him:

I remember, one day that Craig repeated to me his famous "You believe in the actor, I do not",
replying: "I do not know if I believe in the actor. But I do believe in a new spirit which will
transform the art of the actor. I believe in something which I know, and have tested, something
which was established between a group of young actors and myself through daily work which
lasted a year. On that something I have started to build." Well here, in the very first session, I
have found that something between Dalcroze and his students as it exists between me and
mine.

His diary of the visit goes on to describe impressions of Dalcroze working on
simple exercises with young children, developing expressiveness from rhythmical
movements which came naturally to them and carrying through into the making of
primitive sounds. "I am certain", he wrote, "after what I have seen in Geneva, of the
value of a general rhythmic education as the basis of instruction for the professional
actor."

It is interesting that Copeau should have thought of his young Vieux-Colombier
actors as his students. When the opportunity came, a few months later, to make a fresh
start to the Vieux-Colombier experiment in New York, Copeau's company consisted
of some of those actors from that first season and some makeshift replacements for
those whose careers (and in some cases, lives) had been ended by the war. Copeau
made a preliminary visit to the United States and made positive pronouncements
about the task, as he saw it, of making the actor fit for the stage so that the stage
would be fit for the poet:

We shall restore the actor, as a man and as an artist, defend him against the stiffening of
specialisation, and take him away from the dissipation of town life · . .[6]

Yet, after two seasons at the Garrick Theatre, he admitted, in his lecture at the
Cleveland Playhouse, that he had overreached himself and that his actors had, for the
most part, refused to embrace the ideals which he had offered them:

I really think that the great enemy of the theatre is the actor. Yes I really think it. I can say that
because I am working with actors. Craig is not working with the actor. He is working with the
theatre. And Duse, the dear and beautiful Eleanora Duse, says that to save the theatre, we shall
have to kill all the actors. Well, when we have killed the actor, what shall we do? I say we have
to educate the actor, but I don't think it is possible.

The invitation to America had meant leaving behind in Paris the first, tentative
beginnings of an acting school, Copeau's first attempt to solve that paradox by
institutional means. In New York, all he had been able to provide in place of an acting
school was some schooling for his actors – and they had proved remarkably resistant
to it. For example, in gathering the troupe he had been delighted to be able to include
a recent graduate from Dalcroze's school as a sort of *maître à danser*. Jessmin Howarth,

unfortunately, had no previous teaching experience except with infants and was quite unprepared for the pose taken by those actors that would have nothing to do with work that was not directly relevant to the rehearsals in hand. Attendance at her classes became irregular. The crowded programme did not provide anything like enough time for a proper investigation of eurythmics as a basis for actor-training. Her first exercises, making the best of an improbable job, were in mime: use of the senses, the creation of character through silhouette and the imitation of rhythm in other people. All these techniques were later to be incorporated into the work of the Vieux-Colombier School, but with eurythmics proper Copeau soon became disillusioned. When the actors did Dalcroze's exercises to music, designed to develop their expressive potential through the assimilation of rhythm, the outcome seemed to be merely a new kind of affectation, not the combination of natural freedom and acquired discipline that Copeau was seeking.

In such new work it would, however, have been surprising not to find some dead ends. What made progress impossible was not the relative worth of any one exercise against another, but the actors' attitude to doing them at all. In their defence it should be said that their exile was a difficult one and they were grossly overworked. Although American theatre-lovers were theoretically in favour of having the best of contemporary French theatre in their midst, few of them had enough French to want to attend it regularly. In order to provide for an audience that was regular but limited, Copeau found himself obliged to mount a programme that was tantamount to weekly "rep":

The way we worked during those two years of exile simply passes the imagination. I cannot even imagine, looking back now, how we were able to get through it. We put fifty plays on the stage, some of them in five acts, with all their costumes, scenery and properties. During the first season the tempo was almost intolerable; during the second it was inhuman. Twenty-five productions in twenty-five weeks. Two rehearsals a day. Two matinees a week. A first night every Monday.[7]

At the Vieux-Colombier there had been a kind of joy in working to the limits of endurance. At the Garrick there was mistrust and disaffection: from the outset it proved impossible to create the kind of ensemble atmosphere necessary to Copeau's style of working. The actors arrived in New York before him, only to find that the communal house which they had been promised had not materialised: they split into groups to find digs and the life of the company was one of faction from then on. When Copeau arrived he found

everything in disarray. Those who I had left as collaborators in a common endeavour, I now found to have turned one against the other, as if real enemies, and since I did not want to say either one or the other was right, but to offer my goodwill to everyone, I soon had around me only people who were either indifferent or hostile.[8]

When Dullin, finally released from the army, arrived at the end of the season, he provided competition rather than support. Sensing that Copeau was at the end of his tether he attracted attention to himself in the hope of taking over the company. Copeau ran a series of company seminars in an attempt to repair the damage and in the summer of 1918, between seasons, he took them to the home of Otto Kahn in Morristown, New Jersey, the best equivalent he could find to the house in Limon. There he outlined a programme of eurythmics, mime, dance, reading and improvisation. It was too late: the younger actors cut their classes and took off into town to eat ice-cream and go to the movies.

If Copeau had been a raw volunteer as a director of the 1913 season, he came back to the Vieux-Colombier a veteran. The experiences in America had, he wrote to Roger Martin du Gard, strengthened, not weakened him. Not only had his ideals survived, but they had been "purified, strengthened, heightened by adversity". On his return to France he wanted nothing better than to retire to the country again with a small number of pupils and there to pursue the vision of the school that he had tentatively begun in Paris in 1915/16, after his European fact-finding tour and before the offer to go to America. He wrote to Schlumberger:

I dream of a pure famousness, serene and durable, which pertains to the work itself. If I can create my school, I will find the way of bringing it to life and of bringing foreigners to it from afar . . . A place must be found where a religious theatre can be reborn. For the moment that is not Paris.

But the Minister of Culture and his friends at the *NRF* persuaded him that his first duty to the re-building of war-torn France was to re-open the Vieux-Colombier. So, with perhaps less than total conviction, he launched into the production cycle once more and there can be no doubt that during the seasons 1920–4 his pre-eminence as a director was confirmed. But the focus of his attention, if not the bulk of his time and energy, was on the Vieux-Colombier School, which finally opened in 1921 with Jules Romains as Director of Studies. It was never to be properly financed, housed or able to teach its full intended syllabus, but to have delayed its foundation any longer, Copeau felt, would have compromised his position as director of the theatre even further: his work there was only honestly sustainable as long as he could believe the new generation of actors trained according to his credo to be on its way. Then the new theatre (the Vieux-Colombier was intended only as a temporary refuge) could begin. Copeau, no matter how often young people let him down, as in New York, continued to believe in *la jeunesse*. "We want youth and health, and shall use only new and pure elements", he had said on his arrival in America.[9] And back in 1913, when first proclaiming his concept of a school, he had predicted that:

Since our attempt at renovation depends on the actual character and personal disposition of individuals who have already been shaped by previous experiences, we do not doubt that it will encounter strong resistance. Consequently we would like to be able to take our reforms still further in this respect. It is intended to open an acting school at the same time as the theatre, alongside it and on the same principles . . . we will invite very young people to come to it, even children, as well as men and women who have a love of and an instinct for the theatre, but in whom this instinct has not yet been compromised by defective techniques and professional habits. Such an infusion of new blood will later enable the full scale of our enterprise to be realised.[10]

Copeau also looked to youth to provide an audience for that enterprise: the first 1913 poster began with an *"appel à la jeunesse"* calling for help in the fight to free theatre from commercialism.

Thus, of the four categories of student to whom the school opened its doors in 1921, the most important were "younger people without stage experience wishing to dedicate themselves to a career in the theatre" and children. The other two categories, "theatre artists wanting to learn more about their profession" and the general public, were soon dropped in order not to risk contamination of the first two. Copeau now saw himself as the father of an extended family unified by a common belief in a new dramatic order: a theatre community. With the Vieux-Colombier actors, too, he preferred to be paternal rather than dictatorial, but although he loved the child-like in them, he was exasperated by the childish. Unfortunately, that is not a distinction which actors, any more than children, are capable of making for themselves. With both, Copeau found an eventual need to impose disciplines which he had hoped that they would find, unaided, to be inherent in the work itself. He tried to lead by example, being his own best actor and pupil, though he was too set in his ways and too busy to participate in learning the new approach to performance that was being evolved at the school. One pupil was, though, as like him as could be: his daughter, Marie-Hélène. She had grown up with and *in* the work (actually participating, for example, in Dalcroze's classes for children in Geneva) and, after Dullin's defection, she came to replace in her father's mind the example that proved the quest was not in vain. He wrote to Jean Schlumberger: "She is able to respond to everything that I ask of her . . . Her judgements on my work go to the essence of my inspiration. And sometimes I find myself saying things that only she can understand." She herself insists that it was the entire school that replaced Dullin in her father's vision,[11] but it was only natural that she, too, would lead by example. Copeau asked each student to write what they thought ought to be the ten commandments on which life at the school should be based. Marie-Hélène's began with "1. Submit yourself to a hard discipline, never content yourself with little, in order to become master of your soul and your body. 2. Have as your single goal perfection, seek to attain it in your smallest actions. Measure the result of your work only with perfection, and you will remain simple and modest." Whereas the most childish paper began "1. Thou shalt have no other Patron before me. 2. Thou shalt not work for other theatres, which are lowly on earth, thou shalt not serve them for He, your Patron, is a jealous Patron who punishes the ungrateful and makes happy those who love him and who listen to him . . ."[12]

As well as having some ideal pupils, Copeau was also accompanied by an ideal teacher – Suzanne Bing. In New York she had spent some time gaining practical experience teaching drama (as it is now called: the subject had no title and no vocabulary in 1917) in a Montessori school founded by Waldo Frank's wife. There she used games, animal movement, mime and dance exercises as well as different techniques of dramatising stories. The work on animals stemmed from classes that she and Copeau had taken together in Paris in 1916 when they had first experimented with the idea of a Vieux-Colombier school. To begin the class, Bing would give the children some warm-up games, then Copeau would read them a story: La Fontaine's *The Cat and the Rat*, for example. The children would then play at being the animals in the story and the adults would help them to apply their discoveries to shaping a dramatisation. Animal mimicry was of particular interest to Copeau in drawing up the syllabus for the 1921 school because it seemed to lead the way past one of the blocks he had noticed in Dalcroze's work:

the student, the moment that one demands a human emotion from him (fatigue, joy, sadness etc.) in order to bring about movement induces the mimetic, and at the same time, perhaps through an unconscious desire to do so, he lets the intellect determine his actions and his facial expression. Which is an open door to the literary and the ham.[13]

In order to avoid such interventions by the conscious mind during the expressive process, Copeau concluded that the students should work on the natural, instinctive movements of animals, first observing, then drawing them, cutting out their silhouettes and finally finding ways of adapting their own physique to the resulting outline. Sometimes they would then go on to devise a special prop or accessory to assist the metamorphosis. Other ideas of this kind, ways in which plays might develop organically from imitative play, began to fill Copeau's notebooks.

Despite the variety of times and places at which Copeau pursued his idea of a school, there was really only one, and that, in essence, was the one which was already in his mind when founding the first Vieux-Colombier in 1913. In 1916 he first collected his thoughts into prospectus form, and this brochure provides as good a statement as any of his educational purposes:[14]

1. *Rhythmic gymnastics. Dalcroze method.*
2. *Gymnastic technique.* Sports. Athletics. Fencing. On rising every morning, half an hour will be devoted to gymnastics and respiratory exercises . . . An actor, in order to be able to give completely of himself, and at the same time retain mastery of his nervous system, *must be in complete possession of his physical resources.*
3. *Acrobatics and feats of dexterity.* To give the actor suppleness as well as strength, the perfect elasticity and control of all limbs, manual dexterity etc., which was fundamental to the character of ancient comedy, which will increase production possibilities . . . in both comedy and farce . . . to be taught by a clown.
4. *Dance.*
5. *Solfagio and singing.*
6. *Various musical instruments.* No question of turning out virtuosos, but teaching actors the basics of some instruments most often found in comedy or drama.
7. *General instruction.* Two hours a day for the children to be devoted to academic study. For the adults: development of cultural awareness . . . to be achieved not so

much by study, as by conversations and encounters . . . with a variety of teachers, writers, artists, all friends of the Vieux-Colombier. The students themselves will be asked to take classes on a given subject.

8. *Games.* From games, by means of which children consciously or unconsciously imitate all human actions and feelings, which are for them a natural path to artistic expression and for us a living repertoire of truly authentic responses, it is from games that we would like to construct, not a system, but an experiential education. We would like to develop the child, without distorting his development, by the means that he himself provides, towards which he himself feels the greatest inclination, through play, in play, through games which are unnoticeably structured and heightened . . .

At a certain meeting-point of gymnastics and natural play we will perhaps find the secret from which our method will spring up. At a certain moment of rhythmical expression vocal expression will be born, perhaps of its own accord, irresistibly – first a cry, then exclamations, then words. Somewhere along the line of improvised play, playful improvisation, improvised drama, real drama, new and fresh, will appear before us. And these children, whose teachers we think we are, will without doubt be ours, one day.

9. *Reading out loud.*
10. *Recital of poetry.*
11. *Study of the [French classical] repertoire.*
12. *Improvisation.* Improvisation is an art that has to be learned . . . The art of improvising is not just a gift. It is acquired and perfected by study . . . And that is why, not just content to have recourse to improvisation as an exercise towards the renovation of classical comedy, we will push the experiment further and try to give re-birth to a genre: the New Improvised Comedy, with modern characters and modern subjects.

Without dwelling too long on a project and a method which will reveal themselves to us in their own time, one can thus see the point at which the multiple activities of the Vieux-Colombier School converge: gymnastics, dexterity, music, dance, singing, children's play – observed and heightened . . . Let us add *Mime*, the study of the "richness of language", that of all the great French farceurs since the Middle Ages up to the present day, and finally the elements of dramatic and musical composition.

And, after his visit to Craig, Copeau added a thirteenth heading, that of *Theatre crafts*, so that "artists and artisans could grow up in the same atmosphere": one of "mutual education".

This programme, a melding of advanced contemporary ideas on education together with some of Copeau's own, would be regarded as radical today and was astonishingly so in the time that it was proposed. Even Copeau's literary friends regarded it as aberrant: he was never to be able to convince them that justice would only be done to their texts when finer instruments of interpretation had been fashioned. To them, actors were second-class artistic citizens indeed, but they saw the answer to histrionic inadequacy in their support for directors such as Copeau, not in radical training programmes whose efficacy was both speculative and cunctative.[15] Let us look at how, as a result of Copeau's singular determination, some of that speculation worked out in practice. The question of improvisation and New Improvised Comedy will be taken up in a later chapter: for present purposes it is important to evaluate the school's achievement in setting up a new pedagogy of acting.

For just three years, 1921–4, the Vieux-Colombier School operated in tandem with the theatre. Of the four categories of student, only the class for young apprentice actors ever became fully operative. But the alternative that its work posited became sufficiently strong for Copeau then to close the theatre and concentrate his energies on it. As to the other categories, it was never possible to accommodate the general public except as observers of other people's classes; the scheme for children was never fully tested because of poor enrolment and, as for the actors, Copeau quickly realised that he would have to keep them away from the students if the latter were not to become contaminated by the very attitudes he wished them to replace. But, for himself, the working of school and company together was, at times, most instructive. He was able to see problems encountered in the rehearsal room worked through in the laboratory in a way that production deadlines would not allow, even assuming that the actors had been willing (and able) to do so.

Michel Saint-Denis became Copeau's right-hand man (on the theatre side) at this time. He recalls his uncle saying to him after rehearsal: "Did you see them again today? I always know in advance what they are going to do. They cannot get out of themselves; they love only themselves. They reduce everything to the level of their habits, their clichés, their affectations. They do not invent anything. It is all sheer imitation of imitation." Saint-Denis then adds,[16] "this problem of actors' limitations became a crucial one for Copeau", and points to the contradiction between the freedom afforded by the bare Vieux-Colombier stage and the encumbrances of the actors who were loaded down by the dead traditions of the Romantic, Bourgeois and Naturalistic theatre. It was only actors, Copeau noted, that had such difficulty in finding something real to do with their hands. M. Garry with his desire to put a candle out had been expressing a fundamental feeling of insecurity. The stage is an Eden where actors constantly appeal for something to hide their sense of nakedness. What Copeau now sought was an appropriateness of gesture that would not clothe the actors' bareness, but celebrate it. He could see in other craftsmen the kind of strength and simplicity that he was seeking in the actor. Carpenters, for example,

use an economy of gesture so that everything seems in its rightful place. That comes from their really doing something, that they do what they do and do it well, knowing the reason, absorbing themselves in it. The movements of their actions are sincere, they observe real time and correspond to a useful end towards which they are perfectly appropriate.[17]

The notion of real time perhaps held the clue. Stage time does, of course, re-create real time in the mind of the spectator rather than observing it literally, but, Copeau noted, the tendency of actors was always to play too fast, as if somehow afraid that the audience would start to notice that real time was passing. In the school he had the opportunity to see what would happen if they worked more slowly than in real time. Exercises in slow, silent movement brought him to several perceptions about sincere and natural stage action:

There are two kinds of manifestations in an actor's playing: discontinuous manifestations that seem intentional, phoney, theatrical, and continuous manifestations that give an impression of modesty and of internal sincerity, of real life and power. Continuity and slow pace are conditions of powerful and sincere playing.[18]

In the school, then, they could search for exercises which would provide the actor with the relaxation and authority to work slowly and with uninterrupted concentration and focus. What was needed was to link the external action with an internal state of mind in the manner of the unself-conscious child or carpenter. To begin with they tried working from the outside in, that is, from a given action to the "state of intimate consciousness particular to the movement accomplished". In his diary for 1919 Copeau reflected:

The point of departure of an expression. The state of repose, of calm, of relaxation or decontraction, of silence or simplicity . . . the interpreter always begins with a factitious attitude, a physical, mental and vocal affectation. His attack is at once both too deliberate and too insufficiently pre-meditated, or what is simpler and even more serious, not sufficiently felt . . .[19]

The answer, then, was to begin with the internal, with a period of meditation before moving and after, not dropping the inner intention or feeling when the action was complete and thereby casting doubt on its authenticity. Later in the same entry he wrote:

To start from silence and calm. That is the first point. An actor must know how to be silent, to listen, respond, keep still, begin a gesture, develop it, return to stillness and to silence, with all the tones and half-tones that those actions imply.

Real progress was made in this direction when, picking up on the implications of his encounter with Craig, Copeau used masks for the first time for training (as opposed to occasional performance effects) in 1921. At first he used just a stocking or a handkerchief to blot out the features of the student in order to create a need for physical rather than facial expression. From these beginnings came the development of what is now known as the "neutral" mask. The students tried to make their own, but these were too fussy and lacking in dynamism. Then they were given some classes by a sculptor, Albert Marque.[20] They learned how to take precise measurements of each other's faces and then make a positive from which individual character traits could be removed before taking a papier-mâché impression. Thus

8   A neutral mask as used in acting classes at the University of Exeter. "The neutral mask is the exact opposite of the expressive mask. It expresses absolutely nothing. It may be masculine or feminine but its unique characteristic is the absence of connotated emotion. By simply stamping this neutral face on the student's countenance, he can frown, squint and sweat inside the mask all he likes, but there is no expressive reaction. By watching mutual trial and error, the students begin to learn to detach themselves from emotional habit and enter a different realm of emotional consciousness through a precious mastery of the body as a vehicle of expression". (Alberto Marcia describing the work of Jacques Lecoq in his school in Paris.) The Exeter mask acknowledges its debt to Lecoq and his mask-maker, Amleto Sartori, as they in turn have done to Copeau and his original experiments.

each student had their own, well-fitting full-face mask to work with, a mask which evoked no particular characteristic or mood but neutralised the identity of the wearer, thus removing personal preoccupations and placing the resulting figure in an objective context. Their sense of time was also affected in the very way that Copeau was seeking:

The mask lets the need for expression have an interior inspiration, to fetch something, for example. But it then also demands that that gesture be sustained.[21]

Thus the dramatic moment can be extended without breaking the flow of the spectator's imaginative participation. The gaze of a successful mask raises metaphysical rather than temporal issues, even when worn by a novice.

Copeau's students worked first with immobility, letting the mask be. Then they tried simple poses and then everyday movements – sitting, standing, walking, simple tasks, gestures. Then the return to immobility. They at once reported a new sense of confidence and authority, "a power and unknown security – a sort of balance and consciousness of each gesture and oneself".[22] Here, at last, was the way forward that eurythmics had not been able to provide: the ego subsumed in the id, ready, if required, to then select a new ego for portrayal without the interpolation of self-interest and *cacoethes* from the original:

It is said of the actor that he enters into a role, that he puts himself in the skin of a character. It seems that that is not exact. It is the character who approaches the actor, who demands of him all that he needs, who little by little replaces him in his skin. The actor applies himself to leave him a free field.[23]

Mask work became the school's principal means towards such application. But also, for the apprentice actor class, the development of mask works became an end in itself. By 1924 they were able to perform scenarios of considerable complexity and also to offer extended improvisations from a given theme or situation. They also began to appreciate that there were antecedents to the discoveries that they were making which lay outside the canon of European theatre. Arthur Waley's translations of Japanese Noh plays were published in 1921. Suzanne Bing studied these and the writings of Noël Peri, the French orientalist, in the summer of 1923. Here was a form which assimilated and unified many of the disciplines which they had been studying discreetly: chorus work, singing, mime, dance, recitation of poetry, music *and* mask work, all, furthermore, played on a bare wooden floor. Copeau was immediately attracted by the possibilities of mounting a Noh play. "This form is the most strict that we know of and demands of the interpreter an exceptionally developed technique."[24] He entered into a correspondence with Paul Claudel about it which stressed the importance of music in any style to be developed for the drama of the future. Claudel was attempting to work music into his plays as an integral element, but was finding musicians' sense of the separateness of their art an insuperable obstacle. For the students of the Vieux-Colombier School, however, the Noh drama provided an excellent opportunity to apply the basic musicianship which they had been acquiring.

Bing, perhaps surprisingly, chose a fifth category Noh play (one "inculcating the virtues of benevolence, justice, politeness and wisdom")[25] for them to work on. Other categories offer more obvious dramatic qualities for a first occidental encounter, but it was judged that the students were not yet ready for warriors' ghosts, demons or madwomen. The Noh play *Kantan* is named after the village in which it takes place. The Hostess at the inn has a pillow and "he who sleeps on this pillow sees in a moment's dream the past or future spread out before him and so awakes illumined". A man called Rosei travels to Kantan from the land of Shoku – not a Buddhist monk, but simply a wanderer. Sleeping on the pillow he dreams that the Emperor of the province resigns in his favour. He rides to the capital in a jewelled palanquin and reigns there for fifty years. He then drinks nectar and becomes immortalised. Rosei wakes and finds himself still in the inn and that "all was a dream / Dreamed while the millet cooked".

In rehearsing *Kantan*, the students interpreted and adapted rather than imitated Japanese techniques – about which there was, anyway, little information in the West. But the objective of their Noh drama was faithful to the original: the distillation of one intense, otherwise inexpressible emotion. Michel Saint-Denis:

Kantan was done, not in order to re-constitute a Noh, but to permit us to experience, to some degree, its ceremonial nature – a nature that seems beyond time . . . Our performance of *Kantan*, which left the impression of a spirited dream, was for me the incomparable summit of our work in Copeau's School/Laboratory.[26]

Copeau himself said:

I don't hesitate to say that this Noh, such as it appeared in front of me at the final rehearsal, was, due to the profound understanding with which it was staged, its tempo, style and emotional quality, for me one of the gems, one of the secret riches of the output of the Vieux-Colombier.[27]

Harley Granville Barker, an acquaintance and correspondent of some years' standing, was in Paris and attended the same rehearsal (no public performances were given, because the actor playing Rosei sprained his knee). Afterwards the ageing English director, his face red with emotion and leaning on Copeau's arm, climbed on to the Vieux-Colombier stage and addressed the cast:

I have always doubted the legitimacy of a drama school, but now you have convinced me, and I no longer doubt that any progress can come from a school. If you have been able to do this in three years – in ten you can do anything.[28]

It was with such a vindication of this policy from a director for whom, after Stanislavsky, he had perhaps the most respect, that Copeau, a few months later, felt justified in closing the theatre in order to concentrate on the work of the school. That was what André Gide, also present at the *Kantan* rehearsal, had most feared:

He terrifies me when he declares that he was never nearer the attainment of his goal than in the Japanese Noh which he staged . . . A play with no relation to our traditions, our customs, our beliefs, where, factitiously, without much trouble, he achieved an arbitrary stylisation of an exactitude not subject to controls, totally artificial.

While the research into "de-cabotinising" the actor had been in progress at the school, Copeau, as director of the theatre, had been doing what most people expected of him, and most wanted: de-commercialising the public stage by using the Vieux-Colombier to lay the foundation for a new national theatre with a basically French repertoire. "There are two periods in French theatre", Camus was later fond of saying, "before and after Copeau." Now, to the intense dismay of the *NRF* circle in particular, the latter period, in Paris at least, was about to begin.

4   The naked stage

The experiments made in the Vieux-Colombier School soon led away from the theatre as a place in which to make theatre. In the meantime Copeau's public work had been bound up with a building which, to most of his audience, was synonymous with it. His preference was for the "amateur" who went to see the Vieux-Colombier's latest offering, rather than the follower of fashion buying a ticket for Copeau's latest show. At the Vieux-Colombier, the public could encounter poets through the medium of theatre, not Copeau via one of his productions. There would have been no probity in his demanding ensemble, ego-free performances from his actors in order to further the enhancement of his own reputation. As we have seen, his view of the actors currently available to the medium was not patient, but he made no attempt in his productions to disguise their shortcomings; to have done so would have been to compromise his own belief in honesty of presentation. His productions were, nevertheless, quite distinctive, and in chapter five I will attempt to reconstruct some of the qualities which made them so. First, some preliminary archaeological observations need to be made.

The Vieux-Colombier was small, not solely for reasons of economy, but because Copeau had sought out a theatre with an architectural volume that would place the actor's body in spaces that were proportionate to it. The lines of force coming from the composition and movement of human bodies in the playing space needed to meet the actual architecture of the building in such a way that the spectator's eye would be brought back to the action rather than slip on to its background decoration. During his American exile he had reiterated one of the fundamentals of his first manifesto:

What is the new theatre, the new movement in theatre? It is scenery, that is all. And I am most of all against scenery.[1]

In 1922, two American scenic designers, Kenneth MacGowan and Robert Edmond Jones, made a ten-week tour through Europe to examine new developments in theatre. Their intention was not merely to admire the scenery, but to appraise the ideas which informed it. In search of inspiration for the future development of American theatre they made pilgrimages to wherever it might be found – even to a theatre which actively denied their own art except in its most elementary forms. Indeed, their visit to Paris centred on their attendances at the Vieux-Colombier. After their peregrination round the state theatres of Germany they were immediately struck by the differences in philosophies of dimension:

Size is no mania with the French. They do not insist on buildings that are taller than any other nation, an empire that is larger, ambitions and dreams mightier and more terrible. So perhaps it

51

was only natural that when a Frenchman wanted to present actors in a new relationship to their audience, he should choose for his theatre a little hall in the Street of the Old Dovecote . . .²

They understood the practical, not to say pragmatic, attitude that had informed Copeau's original choice of building, as a result of which he was now

creating the first presentational playhouse in the modern world . . . for a long time the most radical . . . and after some years the most successful. But he began by looking for some place for his actors to act.

They appreciated the financial constraints under which the Vieux-Colombier Company was working and, importantly, made the further perception that there was no question of virtue being made of necessity, rather of necessity itself becoming recognised as the basis of the actor–spectator relationship. It was by virtue of this recognition that honest "presentational" acts of theatre were taking place:

He could build no ideal theatre, but he could make one in which his actors would escape the realisms and pretences of the modern theatre, and would play to and with the audience as their spirit demanded.³

This playing "to and with" was the basis of the style demanded of the actor by the presentational nature of the auditorium to stage relationship:

Suppose you had never been to the Vieux-Colombier, but suppose that you knew this was a theater without the illusion of Realism, and suppose you sought for the thing that would tell you this the quickest. What would you see? Probably the steps that lead from the stage to the forestage, and even from the forestage to the seats of the audience. There are no footlights, and so you have the pleasure of seeing the square, firm edge where the stage floor ends. This edge bends into a large curve in the middle, with three curved steps below, and it angles out to the sides where smaller steps join those of the middle on an ample forestage. These steps and the edge of the stage do more than any one thing in the theater to signal that you are not looking into a picture-frame. Even when they are not used, as in *Les Frères Karamazov*, these steps keep you warily alive to that fact.⁴

The picture-frame had, much to the distress of the owner of the building, been covered over in 1913 in order to blot out its gilded plasterwork. In 1919 it was ripped out altogether. Today that removal would be seen as a self-evident improvement to such a narrow building: indeed most directors and designers would regard it as an obstacle to even those illusions for which it was intended. But in 1919 the field of vision left by its absence was in itself a manifesto, a constant visible reminder to actor and spectator alike that they had business together. Whichever side of the non-existent footlights you stood, an indelible impression was left on your sensibility:

The recollection of the Vieux-Colombier that comes first to my mind is of the stage itself: it was both wide and high and every part of it was open to the auditorium. A forestage – on the same level as the mainstage – projected into the auditorium to form an acting area, easily recognisable as such. It was designed for *physical* acting; its form, its many levels, its steps and aprons allowed for a great variety of staging. The whole stage was an acting area, in contrast to that "box of illusions" – the proscenium stage. It gave equal authenticity to classical farce,

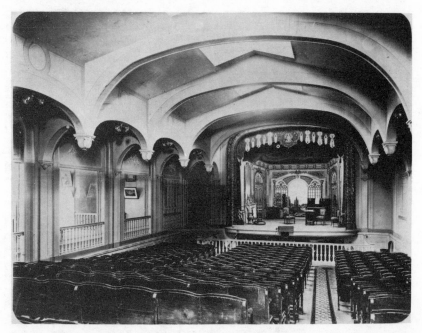

9   The Théâtre de l'Athénée in 1912, prior to conversion.

poetic drama and realistic "anti-theatrical" plays. It rejected any kind of naturalistic decor created by sets or complicated lighting.[5]

The forestage as described by Michel Saint-Denis was not so large in the original 1913 conversion, nor was the whole stage open to view. It had been done by an architect, Francis Jourdain (a friend of Gaston Gallimard, the first editor of the *NRF*). The decision not to consult with a scenic designer was quite deliberate. For reasons of time, money, proprietorial caution and his own and Copeau's inexperience, this first conversion of the Athenée St-Germain did not aspire to be as radical as the second. They knew what they wanted to transform it *from*, but only in the light of actual experience of using it, and of encounters with other ideas and another space, did it become evident to Copeau what it should be transformed *to*. In that first essay, the auditorium was stripped and the side boxes blanked off. Then a small forestage was added, flanked with arches in a black-painted framework, thus reducing the impact of the proscenium arch as frame to the action. The resulting effect was of severe, almost geometrical lines which demanded the complement of organic shapes and vivid colours – in other words, actors in costume. Further upstage, however, curtains were still used to create spatial limitations: these too were to be disposed of in 1919, in favour of a fixed staging.

The experience on which that fixed staging was based was gained in the

10   The 1913 Vieux-Colombier conversion by Francis Jourdain. The proscenium
portals have opened up the playing area, but the effect is still pictorial.

conversion of the Garrick Theatre in New York. Copeau had first been offered the
Bijou, right in the middle of Broadway and only just re-furbished for his predecessor
as Director of the Théâtre Français de New York. Copeau preferred the old base, the
Garrick, provided he could have *carte blanche* in altering its interior. Again he
employed an architect, Antonin Raymond. Again there was a preliminary stripping
out of nineteenth-century accoutrements. The second balcony was blocked off to
create a rehearsal room (also reducing the audience capacity from 900 to 500, but
then Copeau was, after all, invited to New York in the first place as an apostle of the
European little theatre movement). Also the first few rows of the stalls were
removed, again in favour of an increased proscenium stage area. But this time Copeau
felt ready to add to the architecture, as well as subtract from it. As well as an architect
he now had a scene designer to collaborate with: the ubiquitous Louis Jouvet.[6]
Copeau later summarised their quest as a search for a *given* architecture:

A given architecture demands, ordains, informs a dramatic conception and an appropriate style
of production . . . A well-established, well-founded dramatic genre corresponds to a well-
thought-out and stable theatre architecture . . . One cannot conceive of a Greek theatre
independently from the Greek stage, nor Shakespearian theatre separately from the
Elizabethan stage. As soon as the scenic structure becomes variable, then dramatic poetry
begins to lose its footing.[7]

In this search for a proper integration of architectural and scenic elements Copeau's encounter with Craig had been formative – they had discussed the stage as well as the actor:

"There is", he said to me, "there must exist, as there does for every one of the fine arts – and we will discover it one day – a new material, the very material of the stage, which is not words, painting, architecture . . . so and so . . . but technically, specifiquement of the stage."[8]

Another time, he recalls Craig as saying "Bronze and marble . . . and basta!" when talking of this ideal future material. Craig, as is well known, wanted to fashion his infamous screens for the Moscow Art Theatre *Hamlet* from this elusive substance. At the same time, he was working on his idea of a *Scene*, a permanent mobile setting capable of infinite variation in response to changing emotional texture. By the end of his stay in Florence, Copeau and Craig had decided to share the French patent for such a scene.[9]

For Copeau, though he does not mention it in the notes of his conversations with Craig, had been working independently on a plan for the creation of mobile scenic units with the painter Theo van Ryssleberghe. After the success, both public and idiolectic, of his production of *La Nuit des Rois* in May 1914, Copeau's head had been left buzzing with future possibilities afforded by the Shakespearian canon. He at once began a translation of *The Winter's Tale*. But how should it be staged? The nakedness of that first Vieux-Colombier stage had been only a point of departure: *La Nuit des Rois* had, perhaps, exhausted its possibilities. The question Copeau faced during the period of enforced war-time inactivity was how to develop the flexibility of the naked stage without dressing it up; in other words, how to increase the scope of its scenic architecture.

Copeau worked with van Ryssleberghe for several weeks in the summer of 1915 on a system based on cubes. He wrote often to Jouvet, who was away serving in the Medical Corps. The original idea had come from him, and he was naturally interested in the practical working out of its implications. Copeau reported two main problems, problems that Craig was also to encounter with his screens. First, how could they have volume and mass without also having weight, and, secondly, how could they be attached to each other when and where appropriate?

For the sake of solidity, I think it difficult to have the cubes made of different substances. In order for them to be infinitely practicable, I think they will have to be infinitely interchangeable. What's needed from the point of view of fixing them together and the joins being perfect, is a common factor. The first size will be half that of the actual cubes calculated on the width of the proscenium opening. There will thus be two kinds of units: 1. The cubes that provide the sense of height, such as the sides of *windows, small columns, staircases, balustrades* etc. 2. Cubes that provide a sense of mass and volume – right up to a complete wall – *battlements, towers, porticoes,* or even arrangements which don't present anything in particular, but suggest by *simple proportions* the impression that one wants to give.

One advantage of such a system would be that it would allow the repertoire still to change plays several times a week; technicians could still be kept to a minimum and daytime rehearsal on stage would also remain possible. The proposal was to have one basic arrangement for Molière, one for Greek tragedy, and so on. The cubes would be like giant children's building blocks – playthings with which to make plays. But, Copeau wrote to Jouvet,

one very important thing is to find a practical means of fixing these volumes fast to one another and to the stage floor, without ever having to knock a nail in.

They had no more success than Craig in solving this problem. Scenic flexibility at the Garrick was obtained through additions to a permanent setting, rather than through re-arrangements of the setting itself. Jouvet, after prolonged discussions with Copeau, had the job of writing to the hard-pressed Raymond[10] to tell him that they had changed their minds about a number of the specifications that Copeau had given him during his preliminary visit to New York:

1. We have done away with the moulding which surrounded the proscenium opening.

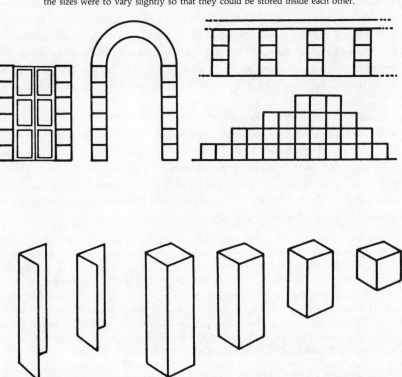

11   The cubes suggested by van Ryssleberghe. The backs were to be left open and the sizes were to vary slightly so that they could be stored inside each other.

12   Louis Jouvet in front of his model of the Garrick Theatre, 1917. This was made
unusually large so that he and Copeau could more easily visualise the effect of the
alterations they were proposing to make to a theatre on the other side of the
Atlantic.

2. We have replaced the two windows situated on either side – thus sacrificing decorative
beauty to a wider and more flexible dramatic practice.
These openings are not architecturally permanent – I mean to say that they could easily accept
attachments on which this or that feature could be designed: whatever door or window might
be wanted. They are little scenes!
     Are the new openings proposed possible, given that a masonry wall would have to be
demolished?
     If not, what openings are possible? Give the dimensions. We attach great importance to
these openings . . .[11]

     Such openings were to become even more important to the 1919 re-construction
of the Vieux-Colombier where they gave a sense of width to an acting area which
was much narrower than that of the Garrick. Cubes, incidentally, would have
seriously limited the available floor space. But there was another reason for

abandoning the idea: a change of scenic philosophy that was the result of one further encounter that took place during Copeau's 1916 European tour. In Switzerland, Dalcroze introduced Copeau to Adolphe Appia.[12] In a first visit they mainly discussed eurythmics and Appia's ideas on word-tone drama and music in the theatre. Later, however, Copeau saw a letter from Appia to Dalcroze concerning architectural unity between stage and auditorium and went back to Lake Geneva to question him further:

In essence, Appia teaches, as a musician and an architect, that the musical duration which envelops, orders and rules dramatic action, also engenders at the same time the space where it develops. For him the art of the *mise en scène* in its present sense is nothing other than the configuration of a gesture or of music made tangible by the living action of the human body and by its reaction to the resistances that planes and three-dimensional constructions make against it. From which follows the banishing from the stage of all inanimate decorations, all painted cloths, the dominance of the practical and the active role of light.[13]

13   Louis Jouvet's 1919 conversion of the Vieux-Colombier. All traces of the proscenium arch have been removed and actors literally had to exit into the building next door rather than the wings.

From looking at Appia's models and designs, Copeau must also have perceived the value of having more than one plane on which to set the actor in space. The design of the second Vieux-Colombier (and the reconstructed Garrick which preceded it) is based on a concept of levels and of openings, whereas a scene system based on cubes would have presupposed a basically flat playing surface on which to stand them. A common problem remained, however: what material to use to build this fixed *dispositif*?

The 1919 Vieux-Colombier stage was more than fixed: it was made of solid concrete. Basta! If the removal of the proscenium arch was a visual manifesto, then the treatment of the acting surface was a tangible one, creating hard, puritanical planes on which to work and be seen to be working. A surface in which "stage screws could get no footing"[14] and which also, incidentally, almost ruinously impaired the theatre's acoustic. But, whatever else, it had no false resonance; it might be unfriendly, but it would not lie to you; there was nothing behind it, nothing underneath apart from some obvious traps in the apron. Copeau was not only making it plain to his actors that here would be no romantic treading of the boards, but was also announcing to potential playwrights that his stage was made out of real twentieth-century materials. The implication was that plays would need to pass the same test if the two were to prove compatible.

Upstage a practicable bridge was built connecting two different styles of staircase, one on either side. The one on stage left led down via a landing to a doorway, the one on stage right spiralled continuously, concealing an entrance beneath. These fixtures, like the openings at the Garrick, were capable of being dressed in a number of ways or, indeed, could be curtained off altogether. But the basic intention was for them to be seen to be there because they *were* there, like the concrete floor, fixed, given. The bridge, like the Elizabethan playhouse from which it obviously derives, provided a revealable interior or "tiring house" below, as well as a balcony above. The progressive informality of the front of the stage, on the other hand, brought Copeau's actors forward into their own era, one in which, evidently, there was nothing to fear from the pit. Through several seasons during which the most catholic of repertoires was offered, this architectural arrangement proved "well-thought-out and stable", needing only essential additions to indicate locale or set an atmosphere.

Décor was used rarely and sparingly, seldom consisting of more than one or two painted screens, or a balustrade, or a draped curtain. Only the barest minimum of furniture and properties was used, and nothing was put on the stage merely as an aid to realistic illusion.[15]

Thus Copeau and Jouvet answered Copeau's own objection to the modern stage which, he said,

such as it has been handed down to us by the ingenious craftsmen of the Renaissance, a cluttered up and mechanised theatre, is a closed-in space in which mind and matter constantly wage war on each other; whereas on the Elizabethan stage, with its minimum of material encumbrances, mind moves freely.[16]

With the "minimum of material encumbrances" of the Vieux-Colombier stage in mind, we can now turn back to the eye-witness account of the two visiting American designers for assistance in visualising the kind of productions that Copeau mounted at the height of his powers as the in-house director. MacGowan and Jones saw four plays at the Vieux-Colombier: a new version of *Les Frères Karamazov*, a revival of *La Nuit des Rois*, and a double bill comprising *Le Pacquebot Tenacity* and *Le Carosse du Saint-Sacrament*. The style of production seemed quite different from the observations they had made elsewhere in Europe.[17] Copeau's work leaned neither towards Realism on the one hand, nor was it Expressionist or Symbolist on the other. Nor was it middle-of-the-road, but a distinct and distinctive style that "used a kind of acting that may be called presentational". MacGowan and Jones take a reluctant option on this word, and it is instructive to see why:

Presentational acting, like presentational production, stands in opposition to representational. The distinction is quite clear in painting . . . An actor who admits that he is an actor, and that he has an audience before him, and that it is his business to charm and move that audience by the brilliance of his art, is a presentational actor. The difference deserves better terms, but they do not yet exist.[18]

Certainly Copeau would not have placed "charm" and "brilliance" very high on a list of attributes of the ideal actor, but MacGowan and Jones are here feeling a way towards a distinction that he would have recognised, that between "performing" and "acting". Actors of *parts* are sustained by a dramatic illusion of which they are part; performers of *plays* by a nothing-to-hide, open contract with the spectator:

It is obvious enough that the first actors were presentational . . . The actors in the first dramatic rituals may have worn masks but they were frankly actors or priests, not the gods themselves.[19]

Or, at least, they did not become so until the audience accepted them as such for the purpose of the play. But to gain such acceptance by "charm" Copeau would surely have argued to be merely another form of *cabotinage*. His concrete stage was intended to militate against such tendencies and his actors did at first feel most uncomfortable on it. Most critics, including Antoine (who had given up directing, but was still regarded by many as *the* authority), saw no reason for it. The first production mounted on it reflected this unease: *Le Conte d'Hiver* was given only twenty-five performances, whereas the reprise of *La Nuit des Rois* which replaced it in the repertoire was to remain in it for the next three seasons. Copeau, however, was unrelenting: he knew that, in the end, the hard, solid, wingless surface would oblige the company to present work honestly. Another factor, not remarked on by McGowan and Jones, was the very narrowness of the Vieux-Colombier stage: it required the actor to use a direct stance towards the spectator; and although he could not be surrounded by his audience (the configuration that Copeau later preferred), he could make intimate approaches via the proscenium steps. MacGowan and Jones likened these to the bridge used by Al Jolson; English music halls often had a similar walk-way over the orchestra pit, and a visiting Japanese would, no doubt, have remarked on the similarity in function of the *hanamichi*, the raised passage-way through the auditorium in the Kabuki Theatre. On such stages the actor can, at climactic moments, come within touching distance of the spectator, not to make actual physical contact, but to make use of the magnetic charge afforded by a closer-than-normal physical proximity. Copeau used such popular entertainment techniques in the service of the text: there was no question of individual actors using them to "charm" the audience in order to enhance their own popularity. If there was charm, it was in the original sense of a magical spell, one that was cast by the ensemble spirit of the company and by the *mise en scène* as a whole.

To sum up the distinctiveness of the Vieux-Colombier style, then: it was a functional, openly presentational medium by which a team of actors conveyed an author's intentions from stage to auditorium, offering the playwright's sensibility to that of the spectator. Large-scale adjustments of this style did not need to be made, therefore, from one production to another:

In the main, the actors keep their own normal appearance throughout; but they are not, of course, playing types . . . except for a gouty foot and a simple costume change, Copeau's Peruvian Governor in the comedy *Le Carosse du St-Sacrement* and his impersonation of the intellectual brother in the house of Karamazov are outwardly very much alike. It is in the mood alone that he registers the difference. In both, but particularly in the comic governor, there is a touch of the presentational attitude which fills the company in varying degrees and informs most of *Twelfth Night*.[20]

What was presented by these distinctive touches was not the performer nor even the character, but (it needs to be said once more), the text. In the American style that MacGowan and Jones were used to, the emphasis was on character:

The difference between this acting and what we are accustomed to, is particularly plain in a comparison of the English sailor as played in the New York production of *The SS Tenacity* and the Paris production – the oily reality of Claude Cooper's impersonation against the rather brash, certainly very dry version of Robert Allard. Allard's performance has the stamp of almost all the acting at the Vieux-Colombier. It is something intellectually settled upon as an explanation of an emotion, and then conveyed to an audience almost as if read and explained. In the school of Copeau, who was once a journalist and a critic, there is ever something of the expounder. It is a reading, an explanation, in the terms of a theatrical performance. It is to a certain degree, presentational, because in every reading, in every explanation, there must be an awareness of the existence of the audience.[21]

All his life Copeau specialised in giving public readings of classic plays, as well as lecturing on a wide variety of theatrical subjects. On his own in front of an audience he would render and link selected passages of a play so as to give an imaginative recreation of a whole work. When he went to the United States in 1917 to give a series of talks, his reputation preceded him; *The New York Times* said:

He is the greatest French reader of his time. He grips his audience, making them shiver and laugh in turn . . . Seated in his chair, he gives to his auditors, with a few simple movements of his body, but with big changes in voice, a dramatic atmosphere such as the theatre itself has rarely equalled.

This sense of being present at a dramatised reading, of emotions being required of the listener/spectator that were not necessarily being experienced by the actor, was fundamental to the tone of the Vieux-Colombier productions. For some actors, Dullin for example, this was too austere an alternative to illusionism, too complete an annihilation of manner in the presentation of matter – not "theatre", in fact. The critic Georges Cusella echoed Dullin's objections. In a review in *Comoedia* he wrote of Copeau's staging of Jean Schlumberger's *Les Fils Louverné*:

The outcome is curious . . . one sensed a sort of constraint in the almost monotone delivery of each speech, pronounced almost as a litany . . . Between *La Femme Tuée par la Douceur* and *Les Fils Louverné*, practically no distinction is made.

That, however, was in 1913. By 1921, MacGowan and Jones were able, largely as a result of Copeau's stylistic essay, to report "a growing sense in Europe that, because the stage is so close to life in the presence of the living actor, it need not and it must not create the illusion of reality". This new understanding of how to distance life by the dramatic *presentation* (rather than *simulation*) of it would shortly be developed into an entire theory of writing, acting and production technique by a young German dramaturg, Bertholt Brecht.

The elements of Copeau's style that have so far emerged could equally well describe aspects of Brecht's epic theatre, where his text is presented by an ensemble of performers as conjunctive to the action of the play, and not to be absorbed by it. One should not push the similarity beyond the point of comparison, however. There is no evidence that Copeau deliberately kept action and word separate as a directional policy. It was, rather, his dramatic instincts which led him to an intuitive under-standing that, although the actor is the vehicle for both, their amalgamation is most effective when left to the active assistance of the spectator. As in the Japanese Noh plays, the whole then becomes greater than the sum of its parts and feelings that would be seen as melodramatic if realistically expressed, can be finely perceived. The Noh drama's sense of the separateness of its own constituents was, no doubt, one of the characteristics which drew both Copeau and Brecht to it. The early manifestations of Copeau's style, however, sought antecedents in his own culture, in the asceticism and *clarté* of French classical tragedy, particularly Racine. It is surprising that Copeau never, in fact, directed Racine at the Vieux-Colombier: paucity of means was common to the temperament and theatres of both men.[22] With the exception of farce, the Vieux-Colombier repertoire came to be assembled more and more from new writing. Little stylistic accommodation was made, as we have seen, but there was some and that was seen to be significant by another visitor to Paris, the English producer Norman Marshall.

The acting at the Vieux-Colombier was, in a modern play, at first sight completely realistic, although the detailed business of the ordinary realistic production was reduced to a minimum.

But watching more closely one realised that gesture was being used sparingly and selectively, so that each gesture was given unusual significance. In Copeau's productions of the classic comedies the acting had the balletic quality which so many producers attempt to achieve though the result is generally no more than a series of self-conscious posturings and caperings. At the Vieux-Colombier the actors, as a result of their training, seem to adopt this style naturally and spontaneously.[23]

It seems, then, that there was more "high" style in the productions of the classics: Copeau was able to give himself more scope in composition and in creating movement patterns which reflected the rhythms of the text, rather than having to concentrate on the distillation of actual everyday behaviour demanded by most of the contemporary works. Norman Marshall further remarks that what he remembered chiefly about Copeau's productions of classic comedies was

their lightness, their grace and their gaiety. Pictorially they were exquisite because of the skill with which Copeau composed his grouping and movement on the various levels of his stage . . . But one was never conscious of a producer composing effective groupings for their own sake; they seemed the natural result of the action of the play, just as the movement about the stage had an ease and fluidity which gave the impression that it had been spontaneously created by the actors themselves instead of being the work of the producer.[24]

The next chapter will concentrate, then, on an example of each of the two types of work identified by Marshall, a "realistic" piece by Charles Vildrac, one of the new "poets" drawn into writing for the theatre by the policies of the Vieux-Colombier, and a "classic comedy" – Molière's *Les Fourberies de Scapin*.

5   Two presentations

Charles Vildrac was a poet who probably would not have been attracted by the notion of becoming a dramatic "poet" if it had not been for the influence of the Vieux-Colombier and the policies of its director. Together with other writers who later became members of the *NRF*/Vieux-Colombier circle, such as Jules Romains and Georges Duhamel, Vildrac was an original member of L'Abbaye, a community of young writers who lived and worked together in a former abbey on the outskirts of Paris. Vildrac's second book of poems, *Images et Mirages* (1907) was printed on the Abbaye communal press during the fourteen months that the group tried to live on the returns from their own produce, both books and vegetables. Vildrac became influenced by Romains' concept of *unanisme*, the idea that collective sentiment cannot be focussed in a single representative type. The poet's task is, rather, to emphasise the dispersive in man's nature, argued Romains: the individual personality becoming merged with the group identity as in a city or a factory. This concept was to have considerable influence on Vildrac's treatment of character when he began to write plays.

Le Pacquebot Tenacity, his first work to be performed, entered the Vieux-Colombier repertoire in March 1920, in a double bill with Mérimée's *Le Carosse du Saint-Sacrement*. Two friends, Bastien and Ségard, young conscripts demobbed at the end of the First World War, have decided to go and seek their fortune in the New World: Canada, to be precise. Bastien, whose idea it is, is a decisive type, full of energy. It is with some difficulty that he has persuaded Ségard to accompany him: the latter is a dreamer, reluctant to commit himself to irrevocable decisions. The play is set in a little dockside restaurant/bar where they are waiting to board their ship. They strike up a conversation with the Landlady and Hidoux, the local philosophic drunk. Then an English sailor comes in and explains that essential repairs to their ship (the SS *Tenacity*) will mean a two-week delay in departure. Since the friends are travelling free (their contract demands a minimum of one year's work for the company when they get there) they have to accept the delay and find temporary work on the docks. The Landlady agrees to put them up in the meantime, and the act closes with Hidoux warning them that if that is the sort of contract they have signed, they will end up owing their lives to the company store. True freedom, he insists (slowly draining his last glass of wine) is not to be found in new worlds: "it has to be carried around inside your skin".

In Act 2 Ségard, who has been injured at work, finds himself alone in the bar in the afternoon with the serving-maid, Thérèse. His love for her is as obvious as his inability to declare it: her response is such as to suggest that a positive move on his part would be welcomed, but he remains temperamentally incapable of making one. That evening, after the customers have all left and Ségard has retired early, Bastien persuades Thérèse to share a bottle of champagne with him. He now displays all the male skills which his friend had eschewed; Act 2 ends with him going upstairs with Thérèse to become her lover.

Act 3 takes place a week later and begins with the lovers eloping "to the North" in the early morning. Thérèse has qualms about leaving Ségard, Bastien seemingly none: Hidoux's philosophy has struck home in him. The Landlady opens up for the day and the elopement is discovered. The sailor returns to say that the *Tenacity* is repaired and will leave at nine. Ségard is no more able to decide not to go to Canada alone, than he would have been able to decide to go without Bastien's insistent friendship in the first place. He finds it safer to ignore what he realises is an existential moment and leaves, a little saddened, an hour early. Once on board, he says, "none of it will bother me any more". As soon as he is gone, the Landlady returns to serving customers.

Jouvet kept a system of what he called *tryptiques* which recorded the setting of each of the plays in the Vieux-Colombier repertoire so that daily changes of production could be effected with the minimum of fuss. On the left, an elevation showed scenic additions to the permanent staging, in the middle there was space for written notes, and on the right a plan showed the position of furniture and other free-standing pieces. The *tryptique* for *Le Pacquebot Tenacity* shows just how little was added in order to create a setting for an ostensibly realistic play. Under the balcony, centre back, glazed windows and a door were set under a fanlight which accommodated the curve of the arch. These were solidly built "architectural" units intended to look as permanent as the rest of the structure when in position.[1] The suggestion is of the entrance to the café from the port via a reception area. The stairs are reached through the door (B–C) into this hall and the first flight is left exposed with a banister added. The stage left staircase (the spiral one) was not used and its existence is concealed by the door to the kitchen. From the plan it can be seen that the bar was placed upstage right, in front of the staircase, with another door situated further down the stage right wall. The only other additions were two small tables, with stools, one up left and another, circular one, down right. A third, larger table unashamedly announces its importance to the action down centre. On stage left, the heavily inked rectangle with the small circle in it indicates the position of the trapdoor down to the cellar.

Vildrac himself has left this description of the setting being struck to make way for the Mérimée comedy:

After the third act of *Le Pacquebot Tenacity*, in which the "bar-room" atmosphere is extremely well realised, when the bar and its glasses has been taken off, as well as the shelving for the bottles, the little tables with their stools and the, rather larger, central table (the one which, in

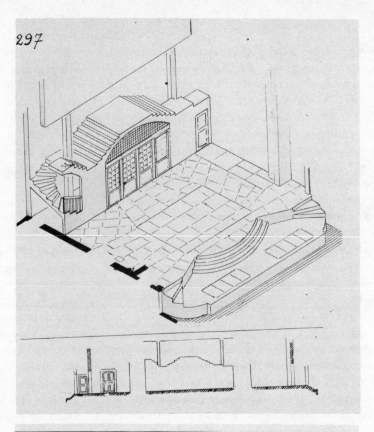

297

Nº d'ordre	Désignation	Emplacement	Equipement.
	Portique.		
	Fond		
	Façade		
1	Rampe	Descente J.	normal à vis
1	Traverse	ouverture, arche du fond.	2 Boulons
1	Entre latte	reposant sur cette traverse	3 chevilles
2	montant avec feuillure	au dessous de la traverse, contre les buttes S et C et servant à la fixation des panneaux ci dessous	à vis
3	colonnes A.B.C.	au dessous de la traverse divisant l'ouverture en 4 parties égales (colonne C avec serrure). B avec 3 fonds) fixées aux trappes et à la traverse	par tenon et mortaises
2	panneaux avec fenêtre	entre colonnes : et : et : et montant	
1	panneau plein	entre montant : et colonne :	
1	porte avec fenêtre	entre colonnes et	
1	porte	portillon du fond :	
	Plan		
1	porte (2 pièces)	ouverture porte J.	posé
1	trappe pliante	à l'emplacement de la trappe C N12	
1	échelle	trappe C N: 2 descendant au 1: dessous	2 ferrures trappes C N: 2
	Proscenium		
1	porte (fausse)	portillon proscenium.	

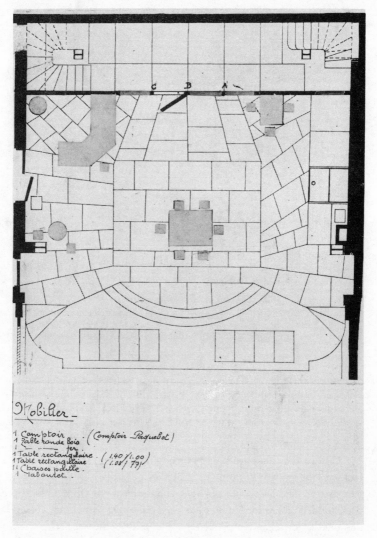

14   The tryptique for *Le Pacquebot Tenacity*. Elevation on the left, notes in the
centre and plan on the right-hand panel.

15   The injured Ségard (Le Goff) talks to Thérèse (Catherine Jordaan) at the big table where she is sewing. (Drawing by Jean Dulac of Act 2 of *Le Pacquebot Tenacity*.)

the bustle of a final rehearsal, Jouvet and I had painted with walnut stain under the amused gaze of Roger Martin du Gard), when a scene-shifter, with one shove of his shoulder, has lifted the glazed door at the back from its fittings, when the electrician has pulled the lamp, with its zinc shade, back up to the ceiling, when he then floods the scene with an intense yellow light . . . [*details of new setting omitted*] everything is ready for *Le Carosse du Saint-Sacrement*.[2]

MacGowan and Jones describe that zinc-shaded lamp, suspended over the central table, as "the mark of Realism".[3] It provided, particularly at the end of Act 2, actual illumination. The main sources of light (and the means by which the stage could have been flooded yellow for *Le Carosse du Saint-Sacrement*) were four permanent lanterns designed by Jouvet and suspended two either side of the stage. They were octagonal in shape and can be clearly seen in illustration twelve. The body of the lantern rotated, thus providing a choice of eight different filters for the lamps to shine through. Crude as this arrangement seems by today's standards, it represented a considerable advance on the use of footlights, picking out the actors' eyes rather than their chins (note that in Dulac's drawing of Hidoux standing at the bar, his shadow is cast *down* on to it). It also allowed for a basic range of atmospheric expression, differentiating between the daylight scenes of Acts 1 and 2, the early morning light of Act 3 and the night scene at the end of Act 2. This new flexibility did not go unnoticed by the critics:

M. Vildrac's work has found a most suitable setting at the Vieux-Colombier. It has been served better by the ingenuity of M. Copeau than perhaps it would have been by a theatre rich in scenic resources. Once again we have proof of the surprising effects which can be obtained on this completely bare stage. The lighting from above and from the side offers very varied possibilities, and I am very much of the opinion that the reign of the conventional and traditional row of footlights is seriously threatened by this decisive experiment.[4]

But in Act 2, part two, almost the only source of illumination was the practicable pendant light. The customers have gone, the Landlady is locking up. At the table, Bastien is reading a newspaper. At the bar, Thérèse is rinsing glasses. The Landlady goes to bed. Silence. Thérèse (Catherine Jordaan) lines the glasses on a shelf and announces that she is going to put the light out: there is no significance in this other than the fact that Bastien will have to stop reading — it is the end of the working day. Bastien (Georges Vitray) suddenly comes to life. He drops the paper and turns round, straddling his chair. With some difficulty he persuades Thérèse to keep the bar open and orders a bottle of champagne and two glasses. Her main worry is that the

16 Hidoux (André Bacqué) and Bastien (Georges Vitray) at the bar in Act 1 of *Le Pacquebot Tenacity*. (Drawing by Jean Dulac.)

Landlady should not know. Bastien suggests how she can be deceived and Thérèse, *almost* without realising it, becomes his accomplice. He lifts the cellar trap very quietly and she descends. While she is gone he takes two glasses from behind the bar and places them on the table. They sit down facing each other, she stage left and he stage right, the light immediately above their heads. She begs him not to pop the cork: he takes it out silently and pours two glasses. As they drink he gently probes and discovers that her boy-friend was a soldier in the garrison and has gone away without leaving an address. When she goes to the kitchen to fetch some biscuits, he makes sure that they sit side by side on her return.

And so it goes on, the audience being presented with a clear guide to accelerated courtship. They begin to share the same glass, Bastien tells her of his experiences in the trenches: out of her sympathy he gains the first kiss; the champagne begins to work on them both, but Thérèse finally disengages herself, clears away the glasses and announces:

"There! . . . Now we say goodnight and go upstairs to bed."

She puts the overhead light out, goes out through the door and begins to climb the stairs, but Bastien catches her by the exposed banisters:

BASTIEN   Thérèse!
THERESE   What?
BASTIEN   Come here, I want to tell you something very quietly. (*She comes close and he speaks in her ear*)
THERESE   Oh, no!
BASTIEN   Yes!
THERESE   No, Bastien . . .
BASTIEN   You are tired?
THERESE   Oh, it isn't that . . .
BASTIEN   Then say yes, it's easy.
THERESE   (*after a moment's silence*) Then you must promise me not to tell. Not to tell Ségard.
BASTIEN   Not anyone. Above all, not Ségard; come!
THERESE   Let's go up quietly.

And up they go, the light on the stairs going out behind them and leaving the stage in darkness.

At the preview the production became an immediate success with the critics. Antoine, the father of French Naturalism, wrote: "The atmosphere is created with an almost unbearable intensity . . . Never before has such a complete *elimination* of theatrical elements been achieved. This demands a detailed perfection in acting. Never before have we attained such a degree of reality."[5] After the performance the author was called for, but he was nowhere to be found, neither backstage nor in the house: a typical act of self-effacement. One reviewer describes Vildrac as "a silent man who retains the ingenuous and solitary manner of a child. His face shines with a great benevolence; he seems distracted but he does in fact observe everything with sympathetic precision. Vildrac, with the patience of an angler, finds treasures in the simplicity of daily life and in the tiniest incidents."[6] Thus, in *Le Pacquebot Tenacity*, he does not intervene in the lives of his characters, but allows their desires and destinies to become self-evident. In order that the spectators can watch them with "sympathetic precision" in their turn, director and actors must make the same allowance. The nature of the text itself puts star billing out of the question, not to mention star directing . . .

To *"decabotinise"* the theatre, it is not sufficient to have perfect directors; we have several; we need, rather, some writers whose work will not allow the least trace of *cabotinage*, Ave Vildrac.[7]

Several reviewers perceived that the success of Copeau's production and of the actors' portrayal of their characters lay in their permitting the play, which at first sight seems rather slight, to make detailed demands on the attention of the spectator. Any attempt to make it more theatrical would merely have emphasised the insignificance of the lives of its characters. Vildrac's achievement is to portray working people without condescension or affectation: the play "has no pseudo-popular imagery, the sort that seduces us instantly by its picturesqueness, but which irritates us just as quickly",[8] but shows ordinary people attempting to establish order in their lives after an extraordinary war. The army had provided its own kind of *unanisme*: in their different ways Ségard, Bastien and Thérèse are all now looking for something with which to replace it. At the Vieux-Colombier the audience watched them look, *reading*, as it were, the production whose "texture and reliefs are so delicate that one wonders that the play – which is such a delight to read – can be just as alive on stage; it is drawn with such precision that its four short *tableaux* assume unexpected dimensions".[9]

Having examined a "realistic" production of a play by a contemporary poet, let's go to another extreme of the Vieux-Colombier repertoire and look at Copeau's "presentational" style at work on a piece which, far from denying theatricality, celebrates it. We have seen how Vildrac's text demanded a certain kind of treatment; Molière was the writer who, above all others, in Copeau's opinion, gives you the *mise en scène* in his text:

he was an actor. He didn't write a word without hearing it and making it active. When a text is fashioned for dramatic life, there is one *mise en scène* which is necessary to it as a work. That is probably not true, but it is pleasant and productive to think so.[10]

Les Fourberies de Scapin is Molière's last work, but not, at first sight, the product of his mature sensibility. It seems to rely on the exploitation of traditional form in the manner of an apprentice work. And the form on which it is based, furthermore, is the very one which denies the paramount role of the playwright: the *commedia al'improvisata*, as played by the Italian company with whom Molière shared the stage at the Palais Royal. And Molière, at the age of forty-nine, did nothing with it – except write it down definitively with an absolute sureness of touch in the balancing of comic dialogue with farcical action. Scapin is the Scappino of the *commedia dell'arte*, cousin to the malevolent *zanni* Brighella. He leaps with relish into the middle of a war between generations and uses the pretext of helping youth (as represented by two pairs of ineffectual lovers) to settle a personal score with age (as represented by two self-opinionated fathers). Standing at the centre of a madly spinning wheel which he himself has set in motion, Scapin takes his revenge on the latter, whilst amusing himself at the expense of the former. Life has brought him experience and *savoir-faire* without any attendant loss of vitality and *joie de vivre*. He is more mature than the old and more youthful than the young. Molière played Scapin himself. Is the play then merely an exercise, or is it a metaphor: the master using bravura technique, virtuosity becoming its own theme?

Copeau played the role of Scapin himself. The production opened the first season in New York, together with a specially prepared *Impromptu du Vieux-Colombier*, based on Molière's *Impromptu de Versailles*. In 1920, on the company's return to Paris, it was again purposefully included in the repertoire, bringing with it the staging which had been used at the Garrick; interviewed on the subject of staging Molière, Copeau said:

Up to present I have mainly staged Molière's farces, the plays with a lot of movement in them, because they are the ones that are least suited to the cold, congealed, half-dead interpretation that is inflicted on them on the official stages.

On their return to Paris, a small party from the Vieux-Colombier had attended a performance of *Scapin* at the Comédie-Française. Copeau noted in his diary:

The performance is absolutely dead. It has no movement and no shape. The production is non-existent. It's 1880 art, without any conviction. The colour is reminiscent of Louis Leloir's illustrations. Croué plays Scapin as a buffoon. Denis d'Inès as Géronte invents picturesque business which has nothing to do with the character. The actors make lines up in order to sound natural. They want to act "modern" and "simple" at the same time as relying on the most absurd and outmoded "traditions", which they execute without conviction or energy, without heart. All that is repulsive.[11]

Roger Martin du Gard wrote in his diary of the same visit:

I would willingly have let myself be seduced by fossilised perfection. But it was hollow, empty. Everything that makes for a sense of theatre was missing: rhythm and movement on the stage, composition of the characters positioned so as to make sense and express themselves with greater precision. Constant and often gross misunderstandings of the text. *Les Fourberies de Scapin* played like this are rather colourless and slow, very old hat, somewhat silly and boring. The role of Scapin as played by Croué is on the same level as all the others. Not only does he have no grandeur, no lyricism, no stress, but he also gets mixed up with the role of Sylvester. They are a pair of doltish servants, twins. Scapin has no relief, no tone, no colour. Each actor has worked out a characterisation with meticulous care and often much understanding. But without any direction, without reference to the ensemble. From which comes a constant false note. Denis d'Inès is an amusing figure, but vulgar, with no style whatsoever. There is no decency, no sense of respect in this house. Croué adds to the text, drowns Scapin's sharp, precise style under a heap of Hum! . . . Yes . . . Good! which destroys all the pauses and betrays this full, vital language which is inimitable. In the great scene of the sack, which is in three parts, the middle part (the Basque) has been cut. Was it too tedious, perhaps? Copeau who had played Scapin, and Jouvet, who had played Géronte, ground their teeth.[12]

By contrast, the Vieux-Colombier *Scapin* was played in an ensemble style, with a sense of veneration for the text and its author, but with no reservations as to the centrality of the central character. In a series of lectures he gave in 1921,[13] Copeau described the play and its title role as requiring "a sort refinement of virtuosity". "There is", he said, "in a work such as *les Fourberies* a sort of joyous elasticity, which bestows, which licences true creativity to the actor." Thus Copeau and Jouvet approached the text with a double sense of responsibility: to restore the traditions of playing it which a supposedly traditional theatre like the Comédie-Française had allowed to degenerate, and, at the same time, to accept its challenge to personal creativity, the platform which it offered for individual and ensemble "refined virtuosity".

The setting which they had used at the Garrick[14] was re-created for the Vieux-Colombier: it consisted, simply, of an actual platform with steps at the sides and back and a double set at the front with a bench between. It was a bare stage placed on the bare stage, a wooden platform, the quintessential *"tréteau nu"*: bare boards set on trestles such as Breughel might have painted in a Flanders market-place.[15] But Copeau's use for this *tréteau* was, of course, not an artistic evocation, but had a functional purpose in releasing the inbuilt comedic values of the text. The roles of director and actor merged. Copeau/Scapin mounted the *tréteau* like a traffic policeman, obliging the other actor/characters continually to change position. Waldo Frank, who saw the New York production, describes its sense of movement, Scapin on the central platform, while his victims scurried round at floor level, "shifting, uncertain, forever in the shadows – waves beating against a rock and thrown upon it merely to fall back undiminished".[16] According to Michel Saint-Denis:

The actors played both on the platform and around it. The younger actors could leap on to the platform with an exuberant wildness, while the older characters were obliged to climb the steps laboriously.

The platform, with its uneven wooden surface, was hollow, and therefore resonant and springy. This intensified, in a pleasant manner, the sounds made on it, either by the stamping, jumping feet of the younger characters or by the slow stomping of their elders accompanied by the tapping of walking-sticks. In the swiftly moving scenes of pursuit, the actors, leaping from the hard coldness of the cement floor up onto the warm, resounding wooden surface and back down again, created a kind of by-play of sound.

There was a perfect integration between the characterisation of the different roles, the "physical" acting, and the acting space.[17]

Whereas the movement patterns of *La Nuit des Rois* had been "curved", "the staging of *Scapin* was precise and specific: it was angular, jerky, violent and passionate – it seemed to leave traces of straight lines on the floor".

17   The *tréteau* when placed on the Garrick stage, 1917.

18   The *tréteau* on the Vieux-Colombier stage, 1920.

19 Jacques Copeau as Scapin, pretending to protect Argante (Romain Bouquet) from the attention of the disguised Sylvestre (André Bacqué).

Over the *tréteau* hung a triangle of lights which flooded the platform like a boxing ring.[18] The action was exposed rather than enhanced by this light, illuminated rather than lit. Like the hanging lamp in *Le Pacquebot Tenacity*, it obliged the spectator to watch the reality of what was going on, in this case the attempt "to re-unite this French comedy with the Italian tradition and to restore to it the violence and even the cruelty of its movement".[19]

One would suppose Copeau's intentions to have been thought laudable, exemplary even. But the *tréteau* itself, the key to the dynamic of the whole production, became a kind of *cause célèbre*, both in New York and in Paris. Some critics felt it to be an unjustifiable eccentricity, a distraction to the spectator offering no sense of location. Copeau, ingenuously, had not expected anyone to take any notice of it once the play started, however obtrusive it might have seemed beforehand:

The *tréteau* is in itself action, it makes the form of the play materialise and, when the *tréteau* is occupied by actors, when it is penetrated by the action itself – it disappears.[20]

20   Drawing by Jean Dulac of Jouvet as Géronte, with umbrella open, talking to Argante.

21   Copeau as Scapin, also drawn by Dulac as talking to Argante.

But, far from disappearing, its notoriety preceded it across the Atlantic and Copeau felt obliged to write an explanatory note in the Parisian programme:

We are not concerned here with a reconstruction, even less with the application of some theory.

At a certain moment in our interpretative work, we felt a NEED for this *tréteau*. That is all. We tried it out and, as a result of it, we have learned a great deal . . .

It seemed to us, or rather we have found proof, that this instrument brings a sense of exultation to the actors' performance, and that it gives form and vitality to the movement of the farce . . .

We were not looking for eccentricity, nor for innovation for its own sake, but, on the contrary, through a certain disposition of the surfaces of the action . . . we wanted to restore its own configuration, its primitive contour, to an immortal comedy, thus re-approaching a lost tradition whose spirit, if it were re-born among us, could inspire the dispossessed talents of today.

That sounds like a lot to ask of one small platform. We will examine a scene from Copeau's production of *Scapin* and see to what extent the *tréteau* determined its form.

Louis Jouvet played Géronte to Copeau's Scapin. In rehearsal, he first found the silhouette of an old man (he was himself only thirty in 1917) and then began to feel the need of an accessory through which Géronte could express himself. Copeau, in a later lecture, remarked that this accessory, an umbrella, was "admitted by the text", that is to say that, once found, it justified itself in terms of the text, not merely as a prop to the actor's embodiment of the character. Géronte opened it and closed it (there being "nothing more expressive than something which opens and shuts").[21] He scratched or tapped the ground with it, he trailed it behind him . . . he twisted it in his hand, then used it as a weapon, as a bayonet, and so on. Going in to the famous scene of the sack (the playing of which had so disgusted the visitors to the Comédie-Française), he was thus armed with it as a kind of counter to Scapin's sack.

Scapin, in Copeau's view, should premeditate everything, like a good director, or a good criminal . . . He could not agree, therefore, with the Moscow Art Theatre production in which, for this scene, Stanislavski placed a boat loaded with sacks of grain at the back of the set so that Scapin could steal one from it when the need arose. He knew that the Italian Scappino often carried a sack as well as a slapstick as part of his personal equipment. (Scappino was originally a thief, and his name derives from the verb *scappare*, to flee – presumably with something inside the sack.) But Copeau was concerned what to do with this sack when not using it: it did not have the same expressive potential as a prop as Jouvet's umbrella, yet he needed to begin their scene carrying it to declare Scapin's intentions. The answer came to him from Boileau's famous complaint that:

> Dans ce sac ridicule ou Scapin s'enveloppe
> Je ne reconnais plus l'auteur du Misanthrope.[22]

Boileau's reference, Copeau noted, was to Scapin (Molière) enveloping *himself* in the sack, not Géronte:

At the beginning of the third act, Scapin prepares his vengeance against Géronte: "I have in mind a certain little vengeance with which I am about to indulge myself". He knows what form this vengeance will take. He has devised it in advance. He already has his sack . . . Géronte approaches. Scapin says to the youngsters: "You go on, I'll join you in a moment. I won't have it said that I let someone get away with making me betray myself and reveal things which would have been better kept secret." So saying, he prepares to attack Géronte. What does he do with his sack? *He puts it on.* He makes a bizarre garment out of it. You would no longer know that it was a sack.[23]

So, with Copeau/Scapin now enveloped in his sacking overcoat, we can now pick up the beginning of Act 3, Scene 2. This reconstruction is based on Copeau's own production notes, as edited by Louis Jouvet:[24]

The two women and Sylvestre go out. Géronte approaches, Scapin tests the suppleness of his limbs . . . Then, even before Géronte arrives, he begins to play his part, pretending to look in every direction for the person he is seeking. Géronte appears, proscenium left. He interrupts Scapin who turns and speaks loudly from his position on the tréteau.

GERONTE   Well, Scapin, what news of my son?
SCAPIN   Your son, Sir, is in a place of safety; but now you yourself are in the greatest possible danger – I only wish you were safe at home . . .
GERONTE   Why is that?
SCAPIN   Even as I speak, someone is looking for you everywhere, someone who wants to kill you.

Scapin has seized him rather rudely by the arm, as if he were gripping his prey, and he speaks almost into his ear, in a muted voice, but emphasising each word.

Copeau often referred to the *tréteau* as a "trap for old men". Here he is able to seize Géronte from above. (Note that Jouvet was a tall man – Copeau would have had little difficulty in grabbing him by the arm from the height of the platform.)

GERONTE   Me?
In a strangled voice.
SCAPIN   Yes.
In a low voice.
GERONTE   But who?
Loudly. Scapin shushes him and continues to speak quietly:
SCAPIN   The brother of the girl Octave has married. He thinks you want the marriage dissolved in order to have your daughter take his sister's place. So he has sworn to get even with you and satisfy his honour by taking your life. His friends – all armed men like himself – are looking for you everywhere.

Géronte gives a little groan and begins to scuttle awkwardly upstage. Scapin catches him and brings him back.
           . . . there are men on all the approaches to your house.
He lets him go.
           So you can't go home . . .
New groan from Géronte who scuttles three paces right.
           You can't move a step to the right . . .
Géronte stops and scuttles two paces left.
           . . . nor to the left . . .

Géronte stops and raises his arms to the sky.
> . . . without falling into their hands.
Géronte supports himself on his umbrella.

GERONTE   Dear Scapin, what am I going to do?
SCAPIN   I don't know, Sir; this is a strange business. I'm scared stiff for you and . . . Wait.
He runs off into the distance and looks left and right. Géronte begins to shake gently.
GERONTE   Well?
SCAPIN   No, no, no, it's nothing.
GERONTE   Can't you think of some way of getting me out of this?
SCAPIN   Yes, I can: but it would mean that I would be in danger myself.
GERONTE   Don't abandon me, Scapin; be a loyal servant, I beg you.
SCAPIN   I wouldn't dream of it. The personal attachment I feel for you wouldn't let me leave you helpless.

Although there is no note to this effect, somewhere here Scapin must have brought Géronte up on to the *tréteau*.

GERONTE   I promise you won't regret it – I'll recompense you with this suit . . . when I've worn it a little longer.
SCAPIN   Listen, here's an idea I've had which seems just the thing to save you . . .
Scapin takes the sack off.
> . . . You'll have to climb into this sack, and then –
GERONTE   *(thinking he sees someone)* Ah!
Géronte quickly opens his umbrella and curls up under it for protection.
SCAPIN   No, no, no, no, no one is coming. As I was saying, you must get into this and keep absolutely still. I'll put you on my back like a sack of something and carry you home past your enemies. Once there we can barricade you in and send for help.
GERONTE   Excellent idea.
SCAPIN   None better. You'll see. *(Aside)* Now you'll pay for what you did to me.
GERONTE   Eh?
SCAPIN   I was saying we'll catch your enemies on the hop. Get right down and above all, be careful not to move show yourself, whatever happens.
GERONTE   Leave it to me. I know how to handle myself . . .
SCAPIN   Hide yourself, here comes one of the killers looking for you now.
Very worried, frightened, half opening the top of the sack. The sack shrinks up.

Scapin now disguises his voice as a Gascon and gives Géronte his first beating . . . Finally, when the Gascon has "gone", the victim puts his head out of the sack:

GERONTE   Oh, Scapin, I can't take any more.
SCAPIN   Oh, Sir, I'm a mass of bruises, my shoulders are black and blue.
GERONTE   What! It was mine he was beating.
SCAPIN   Uh, uh. It was mine.
GERONTE   What are you talking about? I felt every blow – in fact I still can . . .

And then Scapin conjures up a second assailant, a Swiss. This time he pretends to have a sword as well as a stick. All he wants is to "run Géronte through three or four times". At this the sack . . .

quivers and gives a little jump.

After amusing himself once more by playing both parts in a dialogue (at the same time as whispering to Géronte inside the sack), Scapin pretends to fight the Swiss, making sure that he steps on Géronte inside the sack in the process. Then, notes Copeau,

Scapin, after carefully choosing his spot, hits the sack, then turns and leaps in the air like a scalded cat and kicks the sack with both feet. A fresh blow on the front of the sack. The sack retreats. A blow on the back: the sack advances. Blows all over. At each blow, the sack jumps up . . . Scapin yells even louder than he did the first time. He sits down on his backside. For a while, the sack does not move. Scapin stops yelling, wondering if he has knocked the old boy out . . . Then one perceives a plaintive gurgling sound coming from the sack, which gradually expands. Scapin starts howling again. It becomes a concert. While Géronte speaks, Scapin still yells.

GERONTE   (*putting his head up out of the sack*) Oh, everything's broken!

SCAPIN   Oh, I'm a dying man!

GERONTE   Why the devil do they have to hit me?

SCAPIN   (*pushing him back in the sack*) Look out, here come half-a-dozen all at once.

. . . he runs to pick up his stick, goes down the stage left stairs and comes back up again, tapping his stick to the left, stamping his heel to the right, occupying every part [of the platform] at once. In effect he executes a dance. Carried away by his own virtuosity, he performs a play to himself, playing each of the different characters with complete sincerity.

Eventually, suggests Copeau, he goes up stage and turns his back on Géronte, who chooses that moment to poke his head out of the sack and realises that he has been tricked:

One observes a certain agitation inside the sack. A hand passes out through the opening, frees itself, then Géronte's head appears. At first he contemplates the fourberie with stupefaction. Then he wants to get out, but he can't manage to do so. Then he disengages his parasol which had been shut up in the sack with him, brandishes it and begins to carry himself over to Scapin by means of a series of little bounds . . .

These bunny-hops attract Scapin's attention and he turns round, ready to deliver the first blow of the new series, but is stopped in his tracks.

SCAPIN   Oh!

GERONTE   Ah, you unspeakable, swindling swine you! So you are trying to kill me!

[Scapin] makes a huge entre-chat with his arms and legs which sends his weapon flying. With one bound he leaps down off the front of the tréteau and flees as fast as his legs will carry him, proscenium left. Géronte, in pursuit, falls on the floor. As he speaks, he manages to disengage himself from the sack, but then Zerbinette appears at the back and climbs the [rear] stairs, laughing lightly like a mocking-bird.

Thus, as Copeau envisioned it, the famous sack scene would end and the equally challenging laughing scene would begin. Those notes were written prior to the 1917 production, which was rehearsed in eighteen rehearsals, beginning in Paris and concluding in New York.[25] Curiously, then, Jouvet's characterisation with its expressive need of the umbrella, and the "NEED" for the *tréteau*, evolved in some way prior to rehearsals with the new company. Jouvet's umbrella and Copeau's rather recherché justification of his business with the sack are production details which worked for *them*, but which would be unlikely to be adopted as part of a new tradition of playing *Scapin*.[26] The *tréteau*, on the other hand, seems much more likely to provide a key to the *mise en scène* which Copeau believed every good text to contain. First of all, it removed any necessity for realism of setting, clearly stating that the world which the characters inhabit is the world of farce: Scapin has no more need of a "real" quayside than Mr Punch does of a real house. Secondly, like a children's game, it defines territory: whoever stands on it (Scapin for most of the time) is "King of the Castle". Thus in the overturning of master–servant relationships on which *Scapin*, like so many *commedia* scenarios, is based, it provided a physical basis for the new pecking order – mastery of it belonged only to those with superior physical and mental agility. Géronte, when he finally realises that he is being fooled and humiliated, for once gains a right to the territory and Scapin, in recognition of that fact, immediately performs his famous *lazzi* and, literally, scarpers. But Géronte's possession of the *tréteau* is short-lived: he is not even able to extricate himself from it in time to give chase. His only possible right to remain in possession of it thereafter would have been to deliver a raging monologue in the style of Pantalone, but this is denied him by the arrival of another mercurial spirit, the *seconda donna innamorata*, Zerbinette.

The *tréteau*'s third virtue, which Michel Saint-Denis alludes to, was its noisiness. The sack scene, which is the climax of the farce in *Scapin*, outdoing all his previous *fourberies*, not only builds to a visual climax, with Scapin rushing around playing six parts at once, but an aural one, too. Normally one would hear the sound of the blows, Géronte howling and Scapin yelling: the *tréteau* adds a percussive accompaniment, Scapin's feet moving faster and faster as the scene progresses and, presumably, louder and louder as well. His dance round his victim could almost have become a primitive ritual whose climax might have been slaughter – but this is farce and the *tréteau*'s final service to Scapin was as a springboard from which to begin his acrobatic flight.

The Vieux-Colombier *tréteau* was also used for another presentation in the repertoire, Molière's *Le Médecin Malgré Lui*, another farce of *commedia dell'arte* parentage. André Suarès said of Copeau's *tréteau* that it "puts the enormity of farce on the desired level. Neither farce nor tragedy can live on the floor."[27] Jouvet felt that it deserved a study to itself; its real value to Copeau's work was, however, only revealed later when the researches which had been conducted at the Vieux-Colombier School emerged into the sunlight of Burgundy.

6   Retreat in Burgundy

The Vieux-Colombier Company and the Vieux-Colombier School proved incapable of being worked in tandem as Copeau had hoped. Suzanne Bing had more or less given up acting at the theatre by 1924 in order to concentrate on the work at the school. After the disappointment of *La Maison Natale* Copeau became unable to resist the intuitive impulse to do likewise. The "school in the country" project which had been foremost in his thoughts on his return from America seemed now to be the only way forward. He still believed that a performing company and a training school could, and should, have a vital working relationship, but he now saw that it would need to be established through initial emphasis on the new training methods, not continual public performance. The discoveries being made at the school offered potential for a new supremacy of the art of theatre, whereas Copeau's own productions, however exceptional for their time, were merely making limited, short-term use of existing materials. Nor could the school's work simply be made public – neither the students nor Parisian audiences were ready for that. Copeau had always doubted that his renovated theatre could flourish perennially in the acid soil of the city, whether Paris or New York. In the country he could look forward to renewing his own powers at the same time as letting the new work have time and space in which to grow. Furthermore, rural audiences, lacking urbane assurance in their own dramatic sophistication, might be able to appreciate intuitively the performances that would eventually be offered. Some of the new methods were, after all, very old indeed. In February 1924 he wrote to Roger Martin du Gard:

My dear Roger, you would be very kind if you could tell me if there exists, whether at Porquerolles, or in the vicinity of Hyères, any fairly large property, well-situated, with the usual facilities, comprising one or more dwellings (a farm, a manor house . . .) in which twenty-five or thirty people could be accommodated.

André Gide, in the temporary privacy of his diary, despaired of his friend's romanticism: to retreat to the country in an attempt to commune simultaneously with the theatre and with nature was, in his opinion, to go in quest of a chimera. Gide did not, anyway, believe that theatre could be restored as a pure form: it was too dependent on public taste. The sight of Copeau, seemingly lost to literature, inveterately pursuing such an ideal, saddened him:

It is because the artistic ideal of Copeau is chimerical that he is a pathetic figure. I have always thought there was something of Ibsen's "Brand" in him. He too let himself be seduced by an image of sanctity, and much pride lies hidden beneath it.[1]

That judgement was made in 1931, after Copeau gave his *Souvenirs* lectures at the Vieux-Colombier and was, once more, talking of new beginnings. In 1950, the year after Copeau's death, Eric Bentley wrote an article in which he defended him against Gide's acerbity: Copeau's ideals for the theatre were not, wrote Bentley, "any more chimerical than the ideals of any other great reformer".[2] In 1951 Jean Mambrino, with more facts than Bentley at his disposal, expounded further on the consistency of Copeau's actions in relation to his ideals. He wrote in *The Dublin Review*:

We begin to see now the striking unity of this life, its uninterrupted search for the Absolute. We can see how Copeau's mysterious "retreat" was already implicit in many of his former attitudes. There was no failure here, no reason for regret . . . For it was his vocation to be a prophet, to conquer the land, not to parcel it out.[3]

The impulses which led Copeau to found the Vieux-Colombier were, indeed, not so very different from the ones which led him away from it. The decision to abandon ship in order to continue the search by other means should not, however, be assumed to have been equally well prepared. The burning of the Vieux-Colombier boat was an instinctive action, he later said, like leaving home at the age of twenty.

For Copeau's actors, for his friends from the NRF and for the official Friends of the Vieux-Colombier, the closure was a disaster; not natural, but man-made – and that man was Copeau himself. They felt betrayed: his credo of 1913 had been torn up as a caprice. To close at a time when a reputation had been secured, when the war-wound had been healed, in order to satisfy further a taste for experimental opportunism, seemed to be the action of a hero with a flaw that might prove fatal. True, the theatre had been losing money (the enlarged forestage had reduced the seating to 363, thus making play production with a permanent company a marginal proposition, even with good percentage box-office returns). Latterly audiences had been falling off. The Friends had pressed Copeau to move to larger, more commercially viable, premises. Subsidy was offered for such a development, but Copeau's New York experiences had left him with a deep mistrust of the strings attached to unearned income and he had vowed never again to let himself be artistically compromised by financial considerations. He refused the offer. It was, said Jules Romains, "the refusal of the Chapel to transform itself into a Cathedral".[4]

There were, indeed, spiritual and religious forces at work: Copeau had recently become converted to Roman Catholicism. He was also tired, depressed and unwell; above all tired, and seeking a year's respite. He closed the theatre on 15 May 1924, two days after the first presentation of the work of the school. Weeks of indecision were to follow. An anonymous gossip-writer portrayed him as ". . . not easily able to console himself over the blow to his enterprise. He leads a life of resignation, saddened and engulfed by dismay."[5] Roger Martin du Gard had been unable to find him the premises he hoped for and for a while he wondered about setting up in the North:

Some industrialists have recently proposed to him that he should spread the reputation of the classics in the *départements* of Northern France. He accepted. But when they asked him to prepare a proposal, he perplexed them by giving such a devious account of his intentions, that they lost all interest in the idea.[6]

His instincts drew him South, towards agriculture, not industry. He set off from Paris "in a kind of fever . . . without knowing where I was going. I travelled the roads of Burgundy in an old Ford. It was raining. I had the *Règle de Saint-Benoît*[7] on my knees. At last I set foot in a place . . . to which, a few days later, I would lead my caravan."[8]

In the meantime he consigned the Vieux-Colombier actors and their repertoire to Louis Jouvet at the Comédie des Champs Elysées. Jouvet had left the Vieux-Colombier in 1922. The rift which had started in New York had led to a termination of his apprenticeship. Despite the variety of work which he was doing at the Vieux-Colombier, Jouvet had felt that he was "only doing Copeau". Now he inherited Copeau as well.

The retreat to which *le Patron* led his caravan was the Château de Morteuil, 10 kilometres from Beaune and 8 from Chagny, Sâone-et-Loire. Copeau rented it on 13 September. On 15 September his mother died. There were other personal griefs at this time, including the untimely death of a close friend, Jacques Rivière. The omens were not good. The haste with which the enterprise had been set up would soon contribute to its downfall. When the "caravan" arrived, it was raining again, "pouring down, and the surrounding meadows were nothing more than a vast inland sea". The "château" was merely a large, imposing farm-house, situated in a damp hollow. It was filthy, had no electricity and the stoves did not work. But there he was, with his furniture, his library, the contents of the Vieux-Colombier costume store, and an excited menagerie of apprentice actors, "exactly like old man Noah on his ark, surrounded by a crowd of young faces quizzing my feeble looks."[9]

The total count was: Madame Copeau and their younger children, Pascal and Edi; the poet Georges Chennevière (who had been in charge of the literary classes at the old school and who was eagerly looking forward to writing for the new company); Madame Chennevière; Miko and Michel Saint-Denis with their new-born baby; Alexandre Janvier, the technician from the Vieux-Colombier and his wife and son; Claude Varese; Suzanne and Bernard Bing; August Boverio, Suzanne Boverio; Jean Villard, Charlotte Villard, Laurence Villard; François Vibert. These four actors and their families had wanted to accompany him from the Vieux-Colombier rather than find other acting jobs in Paris. Suzanne Maistre and Léon Chancerel and his wife took rooms in Demigny. The pupils from the school were: Yvonne Galli, Marie-Hélène Copeau, Marie-Madeleine Gautier, Marguerite Cavadaski, Clarita Stoessel, Michette Bossu, Jean Dasté, Jean Dorcy, Etienne Decroux and Aman Maistre.

Thus the ark was filled with interlocking family groups, making the school–company division less pronounced than before. On 4 November, Copeau brought them together for an introductory talk. He said why he had come and that he had abandoned everything in order to do so. He regarded it as his last chance in life and they should realise the responsibility this placed them under; their sense of that responsibility would show itself in a perfectionist attitude to work and a dignified life style. He laid great emphasis on the morality of the artist and the discipline needed to aspire to it. He had not obliged anyone to come: they were all volunteers and would have to accept poverty as a condition of discipleship. There would be no question of erasing their personalities, rather of disciplining, managing and conserving their individuality. They would need respect for others, discretion and deference; above all, sincerity, charity, intelligence and good humour. He himself was not infallible, but he would never do anything knowing it to be unjust. They would never bore him. His powers were all coming back to him. He went on to explain how these general principles would be worked out in practical detail in the rules for the school and for the house. He could only work if these rules were observed, since freedom would only come from regulation and observance.[10]

Only Copeau's notes for this speech are extant: as he spoke he may have sounded less pontifical, but it seems that, whereas in Paris he had thought of himself as a father to the company, now he would be Father to the Morteuil inhabitants. It is difficult not to regret the incursion of this religious precondition into what should have been an exemplary but secular experiment in the self-education of an artistic community. The attempts to set up such an order led to a proliferation of petty rules (use of bicycles, late nights, punctuality at meals). Many of the students found themselves unable to accept that, in order to become perfect performers, they also had to achieve perfection in table laying . . . Moreover, poverty was real, not just doctrinal and, after the rains stopped, the damp grew worse, not better. This was not the well-situated spot he had written of to Martin du Gard. Nor could they enjoy the summer days that had graced the rehearsals in the garden at Limon. Autumn mists brought colds, sore throats and rheumatism. Work was frequently interrupted by such *malaises*, especially the vital preparations for the presentation of two new one-act pieces written specially by *le Patron*: *L'Impôt* and *L'Objet*. He posted a notice to explain why the proposed performance of these plays at Lille was vital to the economy of the enterprise:

Important Notice: The performance which we are to give at Lille is for propaganda purposes regarding the subscription to be raised in the North to re-establish the working capital of the Vieux-Colombier. The Morteuil community has in effect only managed to exist until now on moneys advanced by the Directorate. There will be no revenue from our work until next year. The net return from the performance at Lille will therefore be put directly towards defraying subsistance expenses at Morteuil.

Any accountant would remark on the worrying confusion of budgets here: the Vieux-Colombier, Copeau's own funds, the Morteuil community, the subscription in the North, the box-office from the performance at Lille itself. Unlike the foundation of the Vieux-Colombier, there was no sound financial footing to the Morteuil enterprise, and no Schlumberger to organise one while the creative process continued elsewhere. In some tangled way to do with the Vieux-Colombier and the still not dead expectations from the North, the future of the new school–company depended on the success of these two new plays to be presented by actors who had hardly had time to take their coats off, let alone give any performances together.

The pieces were composed by different means: for *L'Objet*, Copeau had the actors improvise in the living-room (their only rehearsal space) while he watched. He would then re-stage and shape the action and write down the dialogue. A "comedy–ballet" emerged, linking sketches for masked characters and speciality turns round a thin plot concerning the search for an object (which turned out to be a jazz tune, to which the play ended in a dance). *L'Impôt*, on the other hand, was adapted by Copeau from a piece by Pierre de L'Estoile concerning a poor man who tried to keep the king's adviser from drinking his beer by drinking it all himself. Madame Chancerel finished typing it on 20 December. The performances in Lille were given on 24 January. Boverio, who had the leading role in *L'Objet*, was ill and collapsed on stage. The audience were, furthermore, offended by the blatant appeal for money allegorised in *L'Impôt*. Despite, apparently, a very good performance by Michel Saint-Denis and an excellent one from Copeau, the curtain fell to a glacial silence. The company's log-book records:

Tuesday 10 February. The withdrawal of M. Eugène Mathon and his consortium from Lille obliges *le Patron* to envisage the possibility, perhaps very close, of a more or less temporary dissolution of the community.

And then, on Sunday 22 February:

Le Patron speaks to everyone, and to the assembled school.
His notes:

Brutal and indisputable fact.
300,000 francs overspent . . .
All that I possessed.
For the time being I do not want to risk my opportunity. I want to use it to re-organise and to do some personal work with a view to re-opening in one year's time.

Deeply hurt. Not at all discouraged.

The history of all enterprises which set themselves a real goal is the history of partial successes and repeated setbacks, right up until the final victory.

Final victory is a question of endurance, of will-power and, if one is talking of a collective enterprise, solidarity.

It is when setbacks occur that the best attitudes, the deepest feelings and the fidelity of those who make up the community manifest themselves.

Those who should meet again will always meet again.

People should speak to him personally, he continued, about their disappointments. He would help where he could. But:

This situation cannot go on any longer.
I am leaving tomorrow.
General departure will be on Wednesday.
Is there anything you want to say to me?

The enterprise had lasted only five months. But though the ship had not been well-founded, or had been launched too soon, it was not to sink without trace. Another aspect of Copeau's insistence on the moral development of the performer had resulted, not in rules, but in rituals: small celebrations by which the Morteuil community had been encouraged to express its sense of its own inner life. In contrast to the artificially inseminated pieces presented at Lille, they had given birth to celebrations of their own life together, the feast days of their own living calendar:

Tuesday 6 January. Epiphany. A *galette* is carried to each of the three tables by pupils in costume; the lanterns from *La Nuit des Rois* illuminate the procession. Kings and Queens are wearing crowns which have been made during the day. Extracts from *The Golden Fleece*, relating to the feast, have been illustrated by Edi and stuck on the walls. A lively evening of dances and charades, Villard at the piano as usual . . .

Such rituals and celebrations had been frequent at the Vieux-Colombier School where "birthdays were celebrated with decorations, dancing, masquerades and games – some of which involved send-ups of their class-work".[11] And those lanterns were much used. When, later, after the foundation of the Copiaus, Jean Dasté returned from military service, they formed the basis of another celebration. It involved "much use of lanterns and decoration of the main alley. The girls in white dresses". The reception took place "as a processional, with a standard-bearer at the front. Celebration and ball in the alleyway with lanterns."[12]

And on 21 February, the day before Copeau's final speech to the community, it had been:

Boverio's birthday, flowers on the table, cake, traditional celebration. In the evening the pupils showed several exercises which they had prepared during le Patron's absence [Copeau had been away, making futile last-minute attempts to raise money] and Yvonne, Marguerite, Michette and Pascal put on a little play they had devised themselves, built round a character Pascal had presented on one of the evenings given over to being in disguise: M. Valentin.

Copeau's instincts were not functioning. Others were better able to intuit that it was this ability to use their skills as performers to create festive atmospheres and celebratory events that was the company's true capital. After Copeau's speech on 22 February, it was Boverio and Villard who approached him to say that they wanted to stay on their own expense:

Nevertheless, there were some among us who could not reconcile ourselves to this defeat. We had gone to Burgundy, we wanted to stay there. In looking round that corner of France we had discovered well-equipped halls in the villages. We should be able – with a reduced company – to find a livelihood in a rich, populous region which seemed to us to be open to dramatic art.[13]

Suzanne Bing, Léon Chancerel, Michel Saint-Denis and Aman Maistre decided to stay with them and from 1 March 1925 a new organisation took over at Morteuil.

Michel Saint-Denis took over as director of the troupe and Marie-Hélène Copeau and Marie-Madeleine Gautier took charge of costume and settings, with Claude Varese (Suzanne Bing's daughter) as an apprentice. They cleaned the house, symbolically, from top to bottom, joking and laughing as they did so, and went straightaway into rehearsal. Copeau offered them his help as a writer and as an actor. He also continued to give lectures and readings, raising money for the work by travelling repeatedly to Paris, Brussels, Strasbourg and Lyon. On 9 May, the log-book notes, "The local people, putting le Patron's name into dialect, call us 'les Copiaus'. The troupe adopts this title." Much as he despised the cult of personality in the theatre, Copeau's name was still the company's most valuable asset. But where it went, he was bound to follow. On 8 June:

Le Patron gathers the little troupe together: Michel, Villard, Boverio, Maistre, Chancerel, Suzanne Bing: since, as it has turned out, his collaboration has become more frequent and more necessary than had been foreseen, and since he has in fact found himself drawn towards directing the work, he judges it more profitable, both for the progress and the prosperity of the young company, if he officially takes on the directorship. He confides his state of mind at this moment in his life; the developments that he can foresee; the pre-conditions of such an undertaking: correctness, collaboration, confidence in each other. He then addresses himself to Chancerel, to ask him in particular, as he has already had occasion to do, to bring the greatest possible circumspection into the expression of his feelings, which, sometimes effusing in one direction, sometimes in another depending on his personal disappointments and enthusiasms, create an atmosphere in our relationships which militates against the kind of work we are engaged in. Chancerel pleads a poet's sensibility and the freedom of expression it requires of him. He protests his affection for le Patron.

Léon Chancerel,[14] although familiar with the Vieux-Colombier's work methods, had never been a member of the company. Copeau obviously felt it necessary to take remedial action as his first step as the director of the new troupe. He wanted him to realise that, as ever in their production processes, it would be good working relations that would set the tone, not good individual performances. On 14 July, Chancerel announced his departure, and on 26 July he and his wife made their goodbyes, taking with them their "masks, puppets, materials, props, books, music and archives". The loss of such an experienced member was, one assumes, difficult to cover.[15] Copeau's son, Pascal, who had just passed his university Part I examinations, found himself obliged to take over Chancerel's role. But, as we have already noted, Jean Dasté had now returned from military service.

The basis of Copeau's mistrust of Chancerel was that the latter was proposing to open his own theatre company in the nearby village of Pernand-Vergelesses, and was intending to take key personnel, including Boverio and Villard, with him. In fact, Marie-Hélène remembers her father's decision to take over the company as being based on a suspicion that the Copiaus were about to turn their back on his work principles. He did actually threaten to take his circle of family and dependants away if his demands were not met. Villard explains how the other half of the company felt:

We simply couldn't understand why he did not take this chance to be able to meditate alone, to prepare for the future with complete intellectual freedom, at the same time as having beside him a little troupe that was attached to him, yet prepared to live on its own means; and, moreover, ready to serve him, before anyone, if he had something to bring us. But he was unable to entertain the idea that we could be independent from him.[16]

The rift would not need to concern us if Chancerel's disaffection were not, at least in part, based on his reaction to the first play that Copeau had written for the new repertoire: *Le Veuf*. This was performed as part of the company's debut at Demigny on 17 May 1925. The full programme was as follows:

First part:

Les Copiaus, prologue.
Les Sottises de Gilles, XVIIIth century burlesque by Thomas Guelette.

Interval.

Second Part:

Comic intermezzo by the three musicians.
Le Veuf, one-act drama.
Les Jeunes Filles à Marier, a *divertissement*, interspersed with songs.

This first essay in community theatre was a pot-pourri of contributions from company members, rapidly assembled. The prologue was written by Michel Saint-Denis and marked the first appearance of a character called Jean Bourgignon, who was to become central to the Copiaus' sense of regional identity, a vivid personality, rooted in the local soil:

> Stretched out on the slope, on the side of the hill,
> Running up or down a furrow,
> Under a sun which penetrates the earth,
> I make myself look, despite the hardship,
> The baked skin and the naked breast,
> Like a king: always fighting, always at war,
> Who knows victory and defeat,
> But whose renown,
> For countless centuries,
> Has held dominion over a certain land,
> For I make Burgundy wine
> And my name is Jean Bourgignon.

Les Sottises de Gilles was a showcase for Jean Villard's speciality act, based on the eighteenth-century performer of the role of Pierrot. In the intermezzo there were songs, monologues by Chancerel and music by Villard, including a march written specially for the Fanfare de Demigny, the local festival in which they were participating. The *divertissement* was by Léon Chancerel, with Villard at the piano accompanying various characters, including Jean Bourgignon once more.

In the afternoon, Michel Saint-Denis, as Tartaglia, carried the Copiaus' banner in the Fanfare procession. Edi had designed and illustrated a large programme which was hung in the hall, which itself was garlanded with leaves. The log notes "Air of celebration . . . overall a success. The play was not liked." In other words, the company had succeeded for the most part in translating their capacity for internal celebration into a public festivity. *Le Veuf*, however, had not sorted well with the rest of the programme. It was a one-act play for one actor — Copeau himself. He had chosen to dramatise a real event which had recently taken place in the village of Demigny itself: an old, neurasthenic peasant had killed himself by drinking, almost in one gulp, a litre of marc de Bourgogne. In *Mon Demi-Siècle*, Jean Villard-Gilles (as he later called himself) asks the obvious question:

Was this a show to present to country folk, the most modest of people, who are ashamed to discover their weaknesses or imperfections? Copeau, to make matters worse, played it with an appalling realism. He was terrible at it. It was as if he had collected together, both in the play and in his performance, all the methods, all the conveniences which he had fought against for the past ten years in his writings and in his activities.

The villagers had gone to see the famous M. Copeau act. As his monologue droned on into an alcoholic stupor, they sat in stunned silence. Denis Gontard, when preparing his commentary on the Copiaus' log-book, speaks of making enquiries in the village forty years later and finding still vivid recollections of the frosty reception given to the piece. The mayor and several local dignitaries asked that the play be withdrawn in future appearances — or nobody would turn up.

How did Copeau come to perpetrate such a lapse of taste? Villard calls his performance the worst kind of naturalism, reminiscent of Antoine's early style. It was, perhaps, an intensification of the technique of extended self-revelatory monologue that Parisian audiences had rejected in *La Maison Natale*. Copeau, when exploring his own potential as a "poet" seemed unable to avoid introspection, using the act of writing as a leech to his own internal crises. The writer in him was almost schizophrenically at odds with the director. And if his insistence on being director was going to mean a policy of performing this kind of breast-beating masquerading as local interest, then Chancerel was right to leave. But *Le Veuf* was Copeau's nadir. As he became more involved in the company's work, it seemed to turn him away from the contemplation of mortality[17] back to something like the extrovert *Patron* of old. His writer was subjected once more to the policies of his director. *Le Veuf* was scrapped. A new piece was on its way — *Arlequin Magicien* — which would help the company on the road towards a new comedic style, which will be examined in the next chapter. But in the short-term, in order to fill the gap in the programme left by the deletion of *Le Veuf*, he quickly adapted Goldoni's *La Locandiera* into a one-act play, *Mirandoline*, which was performed for the first time only one week later (in Demigny again). The title role was taken by Marguerite Cavadaski, newly returned to the company at Copeau's instigation. The log notes that the house was small, but the success great . . . It was even greater at the neighbouring village of Fontaine, where two more performances were given the following week. The Copiaus were on their way.

By August a new programme was ready to join the repertoire: *Arlequin Magicien* was played at Meursault in tandem with Molière's *Le Médecin Malgré Lui*. Saint-Denis repeatedly re-wrote his prologue to suit the occasion. Jean Bourgignon became a local celebrity:

JEAN BOURGIGNON: Do you recognise me?
AUDIENCE: Yes!
JEAN BOURGIGNON: Then what's my name?
AUDIENCE: Jean Bourgignon!

The confident self-presentation of Mr Punch or Gros Guillaume . . . The log, with rare self-approbation, then records some remarks overheard after the performance:

"They're very good actors. We must see them again." The popular audience sums us up with enthusiasm: "Very good! Very good!" Several of them have seen every show and follow us everywhere so as not to miss anything.

After so many teething troubles, the Copiaus were entitled to appreciate acknowledgement. The word "copiau" entered into local slang to mean "actor". Children were seen playing at being *copiaus* – playing at actors playing plays. An unusually extended note in the log shows the actors themselves having to learn some of the lost crafts of the fairground booth player, the (much-maligned) *cabotin*:

Sunday 23 August [Nuits St-Georges]. The time of the performance arrives and we realise that posters and a lantern will not suffice, in broad daylight, to stop the crowds at the entrance to the fairground and draw them towards our booth. They pass on towards the music, the menageries, the shooting-galleries and the confectionery stalls, the noisy, the familiar. Michel, with Maistre and Dasté, joins with the musicians at the entrance to the booth, all three in costume, and they make a loud racket, harangue the crowd, busk, and announce what will be seen inside. This barking really does stop people, makes them curious and, in the evening above all, few can resist entering . . . Some gipsy professionals came to listen and congratulate the beginners, admiring their courage.

During one of the first scenes of the comedy, *Les Vacances*, heavy rain beating on the canvas of the booth was so noisy as to drown the actors' voices, penetrating little by little on to the spectators, umbrellas opened, the storm cut off the electricity and, as the divertissement was about to begin, the black-costumed compère who had last been seen in the Prologue discreetly brought on several candles which lit the edge of the stage and threw a dim light on the twelve feet of the dancers. Actors and spectators kept going to the end, the latter saying: "We can't see anything, we can't hear anything, but at least we're under cover."

The weather stayed the same for three days. The ground became saturated and they had to provide duck-boards for the spectators to stand on. They made more friends among the gipsies and fairground folk who were convinced that they must be a family business like themselves – *le Patron* was their father, was he not?

Thus Copeau saw his little troupe begin to find an answer to a question which he had posed as long ago as 1916, when reading of Meyerhold's experimental work for the first time. He noted in his diary his sense of amazement in finding

all my own ideas, my central and most insistent preoccupation (the pre-eminence of the actor and of the actor's role) in Meyerhold, with all the consequences that that point of view entails . . . The actor, once placed in the position of the conjuror, must use his skills to the fullest extent. Through every movement of his body, every change in vocal intonation, he will try to communicate innumerable aspects of humanity to the spectator, and the vast world which lies hidden in stock types and their expressions. It is not therefore surprising that the word which is being passed to us from this new movement is: *Back to the booth and the commedia dell'arte*. One cannot imagine a greater coincidence of views. But how do we go about *getting* back?

While the troupe were getting back to the fair-ground booth and beginning to release the fruits of their research into the *commedia dell'arte*, Copeau also re-thought his attitude as their writer-in-residence. In August a new play joined the repertoire: *Les Cassis*. In it Copeau found, both in terms of style and content, a happier way of treating the region they were living in than *Le Veuf*. This short entertainment dealt with the growing and harvesting of blackcurrants, expressed in mime, song and dance. It had no plot and no dramatic conflict, but was simply a celebration such as the Copiaus enjoyed at home, for which new pretexts were now possible: regional, agricultural, seasonal. The next harvest festival brought them even nearer to Copeau's vision of the Dionysian: the town of Beaune invited the company to participate in their October celebrations for the wine harvest. This festival was the most important in the town's calendar, and the invitation marked a significant development in the Copiaus' status: they now had the resources to cope with playing to large audiences in major towns, although their roots, like those of the vines themselves, were in the surrounding villages. The new piece was called, simply, *La Fête de la Vigne et des Vignerons*.

At the end of the year the company moved once more, to the village of Pernand-Vergelesses, Côte d'Or. Copeau, ironically, had purchased a house where Chancerel had intended to live and base his project. The disposition was sunny, there were terraces and, best of all, the company was able to hire an empty wine store below the house in which to rehearse. After the cramped conditions of the Morteuil living-room, the doves were able to spread their wings again. And it had a concrete floor.[18]

It was used for performances, too. In 1942, Copeau reminisced in an article he wrote for *Le Figaro*:

Before it leaves the village, the white trace of the road runs along the front of a long building which is pierced by a carriage entrance in the middle, together with ten smaller openings, under a steeply pitched roof. This is the wine store . . . which, in those days, was filled with vital activity, when those up-and-coming young actors held court between its four walls . . . A rudimentary stage was erected. School-room benches were set out, together with a scattering of chairs and stools. And along the road and down the path, the whole village turned out to see them.

But it was not that easy. At first the villagers were suspicious – to them a troupe of actors could mean rogues and vagabonds against whose coming they would have to lock up their chickens and rabbits. But once they became known, the Copiaus were accepted; offers of accommodation were made, and they were able to set up workshops in an empty house in the middle of the village. From his study, where he worked every morning, *Le Patron* could see the wine store. From the wine store, the actors could see the hill on which the village lies. As they worked they felt that "the surrounding vineyards were listening"[19] and, since they of course rehearsed outdoors as much as possible, children and old men would often come along. A new school was started, under the supervision once more of Suzanne Bing. And the actors themselves went back to school: in the mornings they concentrated on gymnastics and physical training, often under Copeau's guidance, or developed their mask and mime skills. In the evenings they would often "wear" their characters, particularly the masked ones, seeing how it felt to "live" them as they went about necessary tasks. And also in the evenings, Copeau would read to them, often, again, from literature that had nothing to do with the work in hand: a serialisation of *Don Quichote*, for example.

In his work as their director, however, he moved further and further away from his earlier insistence on the supremacy of the theatrical values of the text, towards a theory of action as the paramount dramatic statement. Apart from *L'Ecole des Maris*, added to the repertoire for reasons that were more to do with the development of the company as a troupe of *farceurs* than to do with respect for Molière as a "poet", the texts, including Copeau's own, had little value except as action. In 1930 he made the simplest possible statement of the corporality of this evolved attitude:

The thing which has dominated my work is never to submit myself to any *a priori*. There has always been, in whatever I have done, an intimate mixture of intellectual operation and actual experience. It is thus that, after years of working with actors, I have come to the conviction that the problem of the actor is, at base, a corporeal problem. The actor is standing on the stage.[20]

That stage was, inevitably, Scapin's *tréteau*: four collapsible rostra fastened together, with steps leading down on all four sides. Those steps could become benches on which to sit for intimate dialogue, whereas exits and entrances were often made more dynamic by ignoring them altogether and bounding or tumbling from one level to the other. The *tréteau* itself was no longer an anti-illusionistic theatrical device, it was a theatre in itself. For the Copiaus (and their successor company, the Compagnie des Quinze) there was no need for permanent staging to declare the honesty and integrity of the varieties of style they might use in performance, since they were obviously only standing on something which they had brought with them. In fact, the very business of transporting, erecting and dismantling the *tréteau* became part of the total dramatic action, the incursion of the dream reality of theatre into the mundanity of the waking world. And when the Copiaus again found

22   The logo of the Vieux-Colombier, later adopted by the Copiaus.

themselves performing in a large theatre they established for themselves their right to be there by, once more, setting up their stage on the stage, but this time as part of the actual performance:

The first time we found ourselves back in the auditorium of a big city was in Basle in 1926, with *L'Illusion* . . . We showed the actors stopping as they sang in a village square, playing as they put up their stage. And the play, or rather the mystery, then took place with its masks, a little music, some ghosts, an old peasant, a witch, a princess, some murderers and some demons. At last the dream faded, the little troupe rolled up its cloths and its curtains, collected up its props and departed, singing its song again, for which Jean Villard wrote the music:

> We picked up a pair of turtle-doves
> From a street in San Miniato.[21]
> We fixed a pair of turtle-doves
> Over the top of our lintel.
>
> We carried a pair of turtle-doves
> On our voyage across the seas.
> We made a nest for a pair of old turtle-doves
> On the dark façade of an old château.
>
> We still have our pair of turtle-doves
> Half-way up a laughing hillside.
> Our children will see our pair of turtle-doves
> Peck the wicker-work on their cradles.
>
> Now, when we perform, our pair of turtle-doves
> Flutter over our *tréteau*.
> And, when we die, our pair of turtle-doves
> Will perch upon our tomb.[22]

7   The new *commedia*

The genre that the Burgundian explorers most wished to discover was known to them as "la comédie nouvelle". Although the *commedia dell'arte* was thought to be its main source, it might have other possible tributaries, notably in medieval farce.[1] Three of the plays that Copeau scripted for the Copiaus during their four-year sojourn in Burgundy were based on the *commedia*: *Arlequin Magicien, L'Illusion* and *L'Anconitaine* were all adapted by him from originals which had themselves attempted to typify in written form the essence of the improvised comedies. As we have already seen with the Copiaus' *divertissements*, these *commedia*-inspired pieces are so different in style from the introspective realism of Copeau's own original creations as to seem the product of another, altogether happier mind. He came to the *commedia* through a study of Molière:

Molière had something ready to hand, a precedent, a *comedic substance*, behind him. He uses it in his endeavours both as a point of attack, and of departure. Recipes were handed down to him which he needed only to make use of in order to bring them to a point of perfection . . . The comedy, or rather the *theatre* he had before him – the theatre of the Italians – had been extant for so long, had reached such a point of development that, if taken as a *starting-point*, any surpassing of it would at once constitute greatness.[2]

But whereas for Molière the adoption of the *commedia* had simply been a matter of good horticulture, making use of the best available stock, Copeau had no living tradition on which to make a graft:

We are not in the same situation *vis-à-vis* the old Franco-Italian farce, nor even *vis-à-vis* Molière, as the one in which Molière found himself *vis-à-vis* the ancient farceurs . . .[3]

If the tradition were to be given new life, it would have to be through a natural process of re-discovery of the roots which informed it, not through artificial resuscitation. Since it was not a literary form that was being re-created, scholarship alone would be insufficient as a propagator. As an antidote to bookishness, Copeau felt that the half-mask might provide a starting-point for his actors in the same way that the full-face masks of Greek tragedy and the Japanese Noh plays had brought a physical understanding to the quest for the sincerity required to play serious drama. The first such mask to be used was worn by Sylvestre in *Scapin*, but only as a disguise (see illustration 19). Copeau's interest in *commedia* pre-dates the production of *Scapin*. On 21 January 1916, André Gide noted in his diary:

Spent the afternoon at the *NRF* with Copeau . . . We discussed at length the possibility of forming a small troupe of actors, with enough intelligence, ability and training, to be able to improvise on a given scenario, to be capable of reviving the *commedia dell'arte* in the Italian style, but with new stock characters: the bourgeois, the nobleman, the wine merchant, the suffragette, would replace *Arlequin, Pierrot* and *Colombine*. Each one of these characters would have its own costume and way of speaking, walking and thinking. And each of the actors would only impersonate one such character, and would never change from it, but would enrich and amplify it continually. If this project were to get off the ground, I can see it needing, and I would welcome this, a complementary theatre, one which would both excite and exalt the performer.[4]

Shortly after this encounter, Copeau began a new notebook devoted to the possibility of creating such a new *commedia*:

It's a very simple idea. I saw the full implication of it one evening in the course of a conversation with some friends.[5] Choose from the company the six or eight actors most appropriate to such an enterprise, the ones with the most go in them, the most self-confident, and the best assorted ensemble — who would henceforth dedicate themselves almost entirely to improvisation. A genuine brotherhood: the *farceurs* of the Vieux-Colombier. Each actor would light upon a single character from this new *commedia*. He would make it his own property. He would feed it. Fatten it from the substance of his own being, identify with it, think of it at all times, live with it, giving things to it, not only from his own personality, external mannerisms and physical peculiarities, but also from his own ways of feeling, of thinking, his temperament, his outlook, his experience, letting it profit from his reading, as well as growing and changing with him.[6]

Typically, Copeau immediately began, then, to think in terms of total personal dedication: in this case of the individual actor to one specific role. And, in order to make such a demand, he foresaw, with equal immediacy, that he would have to dedicate himself, also:

First of all I will play the role of poet *vis-à-vis* these *farceurs*. This new work will spring from me. I know what its origin will be and its first development. So that they retain their freshness of approach, I will forbid the actors to research. The lessons of the past, the common inheritance of tradition, will filter through me to them, in the amount that I think necessary, salutary. The characters first, individually. Then the scenarios.[7]

Gradually, he anticipated, the characters would take on their own life, emancipate themselves from him. Then they would be ready to create their own scenarios and to play them in public.

Although the idea seemed a simple one, putting it into practice was to remain a preoccupation that could only be afforded sporadic attention. By 1935, despite several essays, at the Vieux-Colombier, at the school and, above all, with the Copiaus, those new characters had still proved elusive, their collective comedy still not fully incarnate. Those that had been found seemed to lack the universality of their *commedia* forebears:

Those original stock characters, so strongly drawn as they are, were like the delegated representatives of the humours, morals, classes, professions, passions and vices of all Italy, and even beyond its frontiers. Even though they were but few of them, they could engage in every imaginable situation, and actually play out, in every significant aspect, the comedy of the world.[8]

But even Arlequin, Colombine and Pierrot (to mention just those characters picked out by Gide) had lost their universality, having become sentimentalised by the eighteenth century and turned into a spectacle by the nineteenth. Little by little, said Copeau, their comedy had been sterilised, so that the present task was not to revive them, so much as to re-populate their stage.

As long as it stayed on the horizon, the new *commedia* project could be seen to be one of predominant importance. But when individual aspects of it were brought to the fore, their implementation posed problems to which only partial solutions could be found. Where, for example, to find these six to eight actors with a flair for improvisation and the willingness to dedicate their careers (indeed, their lives) to "re-populating" the comedic stage? And even if they could be found individually, there was no guarantee that those individuals would be able to create a brotherhood such as Copeau believed would be necessary to the proper interaction of their characters. To have a proper feeling for the social morality of comedy, it would be necessary for this hypothetical troupe of farceurs to base its work on good internal relations. Dullin, for one, in his wartime correspondence with Copeau, had evinced great excitement over the idea of a new *commedia*; he even began devising improvised troop entertainments with four fellow soldiers, at least three of whom, although only amateurs, seemed to him to have the qualities he knew Copeau to be searching for.[9]

In 1916 Copeau, too, spotted some of the qualities he was looking for; again the performers were not professional actors, but circus clowns. He went five times, with Gide, to the Cirque Medrano

to see the same clowns again . . . I could watch them properly. There is one, whose name I don't know, a Portuguese "Augusta", who I would perhaps engage in my troupe of *farceurs*.[10]

There was also an English juggler who fascinated Copeau with his ability to vary the timing of his act every night, alive to the most subtle nuances and variations required by the feel of different audiences. And there were the Fratellini Brothers, whom Copeau was later to invite to teach clowning as part of the Vieux-Colombier School curriculum. His first encounter with them was backstage after a performance, where he questioned them further about their facility for ensemble playing:

The Fratellini father had been an acrobat in the old Hippodrome in Paris. He had four young sons of his own who swarmed round his legs and whom he presented to me. He and his two brothers invent their material together. Their turns do not take them very long to prepare. It is the fact that they are accustomed to working together which gives them their verve. "We are continually making things up", he said. "We only have to make an eye-signal. Immediately we understand each other." He repeated several times: "We are artists." And he spoke to me with conviction, but very simply, about the basic principles of his art: movement, rhythm and precision.[11]

This encounter intensified Copeau's sense of purpose. To a limited extent he was himself able to work in future with his own family,[12] but, since he had no traditions to pass on to them, it might well be that a devoted brotherhood might provide a better

23   The Fratellini Brothers in their dressing-room.

working base than one restricted to relations only. This *confrèrie* would have to improvise and play together, to find substitutes for their having grown up separately, and this might also be the very process by which the threads of the lost tradition could be re-found and picked up once more. Much as he enjoyed the clowns and their own evident enjoyment of what they were doing, much as he admired their physical training and respected their living traditions, he was conscious of the limitations of their act: ". . . there is, after all", he wrote, "something routine in what they do and one feels that they could be even more extraordinary."[13] His brotherhood of actors would need to acquire commensurate skills, but that would only be their point of departure: the new *commedia* would be made from them, it did not consist of them. On returning to Limon, he wrote in his new notebook:

The creation of a brotherhood of actors. I fully realised from the beginning that that was the problem. Men living together, working together, playing together. But I had forgotten that other word, towards which I was inevitably being drawn: *creating* together, inventing their plays together. The little that I had already realised was leading me there.

Early in 1917, his correspondence with Louis Jouvet helped him to define further what was needed. But it did not solve the problem of who the new troupe would actually comprise – other than Jouvet himself, who was immediately fired by Copeau's enthusiasm for the project. His letters brought another aspect of the search to the fore: improvisation itself. What techniques would they use, and what bases would be improvised upon? Jouvet:

Do you not think that *pantomime* would be an interesting preliminary exercise? . . . It seems to me that it would be a very fertile method! And at the same time it would break up the effort of improvisation – improvisation which itself feeds as much on the miming of one's fellow actor as on the text which he devises . . .

No, said Copeau. In his opinion mime proper was a separate language; not a reinforcement of speech, but an alternative to it.

Miming words, imitating speech through gestures, miming according to words murmured internally and sometimes with the help of a silent movement of the lips, is bad miming. Thus the exterior expression of the face and the body must be developed in improvisation at the same time as in speech. Put pantomime aside. It does not express the same things. It is an art which is sufficient to itself. I can imagine an art of pantomime, an art of gesture, which would need complete renovation, which would have nothing in common with gesticulation accompanied by speech.[14]

Jouvet then suggested using scenes from existing plays as a base:

Read a scene once to the actors – and then have them play it on its own, without losing its through-line. Let them embroider . . . There are plenty of scenes from fairground booth plays and also in typical scenes from Molière – the scene with M. Dimanche, for example – that's a great one for developing the gift of the gab – one would first copy the scene, imitate it after a preliminary reading . . .

"No. No." wrote Copeau:

To improvise on one's memory of reading, in the name of an exercise, is to practise the method which is most likely to cut the actor off from any inspiration which he is capable of. He would only be trying to *remember*, not to *invent* at all. He would be intimidated by his recollection of the text. Above all by a Molière text, where the language is so irreplaceable . . . "Copying", "imitating" is what must never happen.

Jouvet replied that if it were not good for the actor to improvise after a given text, it might be good for the text, particularly the text of Molière plays such as *Scapin*, and classic texts which had lost their impact through becoming too well known. Copeau agreed (and later frequently used improvisation techniques in rehearsal), but this latest suggestion of Jouvet's was leading away from the subject at hand: the new *commedia* and the resources appropriate to its construction. Having lost the first point, Jouvet now turned to a second, which was, he said, his central preoccupation of the moment:

the joy of my joys – and the hope of my hopes. For I shall be one of these *farceurs*, shall I not? Indubitably. I want to be a *farceur* and I shall be only a *farceur*. Well, I am going to tell you everything I think on the subject if I, completely unaided, which is not possible anyway, if I were to discover for myself a modern farce style . . .

To find his personal contemporary *farceur*, Jouvet proposed a kind of ardent research, tracing the lineage of comic types, including puppets, through the ages so as to be able to model present-day offspring from their ancestral line. He himself was especially interested in the type of the ingenuous old man. Again, his idea seemed to help Copeau advance along a *via negativa*: "No", he wrote, this time in the special notebook:

Jouvet's fervour is carrying him away, away from the point. He wants to undertake too much and through methods which are not direct, alive. I must make him understand that that which must come *first* in the search for the characters in question, is qualities, the personal attributes and the direct observation of reality. The given attributes are those of the actor, with his physique, his capabilities, his actual nature as a human being. Scientific research, genealogical study, will only come later in order to redress, enrich and reinforce the style. First of all, discovery, not apprenticeship.

The first opportunity to make such discoveries did not come until the retreat in Morristown, between New York seasons, in the summer of 1918. We have already seen that conditions for experimentation were not then ideal, but, as always, Copeau was determined to press on with his search. On 16 June he noted, in his diary, for later transmission into the "little black book":

Exercises: Observation of animals
Series of postures. *Sustaining* each of these postures separately. Making sketches of them. Analysing them on film.
Complete gymnastic exercise of the whole body. Analogy with the treatment of the mask (muscles of the face). Example of the marionette. In extreme genres, in tragedy and in farce (I know it in particular in farce) the attitude, the facial and corporeal expression, should always be pushed to the extreme. Neither of them should be indifferent. And the *time* between each

posture well observed. (Muscular timing as in pure acrobatic exercise.) Return to the preceding posture after each expressive movement. That's what clowns and eccentrics do so well. (Observation of a robin on the lawn of Cedar Court.)
In the new *commedia*, bringing together, according to type, certain characters with certain animal forms.

Apart from his reading of Ruzzante, I have been unable to discover what researches Copeau was able to make at this time into the *commedia dell'arte* proper. Duchartre's comprehensive *La Comédie Italienne*, for example, was not published until 1924. Yet here, whether through learning or through intuition, he came, in 1918, upon one of the essential keys to building a *commedia* character. Pantalone, the *Magnifico*, has, for example, to be modelled on the movements of a chicken if the key to the mask is to be found. But Copeau had not yet even begun to explore the possibilities of the half-mask: he seems not even to have considered wearing one as Scapin. Even so, that robin on the lawn might have led to some remarkable discoveries in the search for new *commedia* forms, had there been but time to pursue them.

That time was not available until after the war, in the Vieux-Colombier School, where Copeau was able to see some possible new *commedia* characters take shape. Despite the reservations he had expressed to Jouvet, the students were given types taken from Molière or from well-known literary sources to use as a working base. They would then first develop the externals of the character, finding its silhouette or characteristic posture. Then they gradually developed idiosyncratic movements or mannerisms of the character by working with isolations. By exaggerating and adding to these movements they built up *lazzi*, sequences of stock business in *commedia* style.

La Rochefocauld's character of Menalque, for example, is described as forgetful, and automatic, with a mania for using objects in zany ways. A *lazzi* developed for him was that when he asked for three eggs and was given four, he threw one egg over his shoulder. Other characters the students created were a timid hairdresser, a rich bourgeois lady, and a myopic Polish woman.[15]

At the same time, the students were taking regular lessons from the Fratellini Brothers and were also learning basic acrobatics. The best ones became a school in the sense of a school of painters: they shared a common means of expression, and were committed to it. They were not, however, nor could they yet aspire to be, the brotherhood that Copeau had postulated. At the end of the day, they were still pupils, and the characters they had created were apprentice works. But with the advent of the Copiaus, *le Patron* was provided with laboratory conditions that were as nearly appropriate to the full experiment as he was ever likely to find. Indeed, according to Léon Chancerel, one of the principal reasons for the closure of the Vieux-Colombier was that Copeau wanted to concentrate exclusively on the development of the new *commedia*. The actors he asked to go with him to Burgundy were chosen with this in mind:

It was largely in order to create this form of theatre . . . that he wanted to leave and take with him some apprentices and some people like Jean Villard, Suzanne Bing, Auguste Boverio and

24   Jean Dasté as César rehearsing in front of the doors of the wine-store.

myself, who would have furnished the stock characters, as in the *commedia dell'arte*, of this [new] comedy.[16]

We should look, then, at some of the characters that these and other Copiaus discovered, and see how they were woven into the plays created by the company. Chancerel himself was preparing the traditional role of the Doctor for *Arlequin Magicien* when he left the troupe. He was also developing a new *commedia* character: Sebastien Congre, "archivist, timid paleographer, molly-coddled and ridiculous".[17] On leaving, Sebastien left too. A later letter to Copeau reveals how actor and character found that they continued to relate to one another, even without Copeau to oversee the progress of their relationship:

For the moment I mainly hear him speaking monologues, scraps of which I can get down before he breaks off. I only have to raise my voice for him to go away, sometimes grousing, sometimes sneering, sometimes covering himself up, both with his prattle and his antiquated dressing-gown. At present he stays in front of the mirror a lot, leaning on his elbows, day-dreaming. I caught him the other day looking at a picture of Sebastien aged seven.[18]

Jean Villard's *commedia* character was, as we have seen, a type of Pierrot, based on the interpretation of the character by the eighteenth-century actor, Gilles. In the duo "Gilles et Julien" he continued with the character when he and Aman Maistre broke from the Compagnie des Quinze in 1932.

The log entry for 26 July 1925 notes "Dasté is modelling his mask for Arlequin. Pantalon [Copeau] is also masked. Maïène researches the make-up for Pierrot, using Deburau's formula, she makes up cream and powder. Villard tries it out for Pedrolino." There is, however, no record of Villard developing a "new" character. Dasté, on the other hand, created César, "an old 'quacker' with a keen nose for business". Boverio had a Lord Quick, a "thoughtless, fat old man, who delighted in recalling his entire past life, both literary and worldly". As well as Jean Bourgignon, Michel Saint-Denis developed Oscar Knie, a violent character who made great demands on him and became a parasite on his own personality. He started from a

25 Michel Saint-Denis as Knie, rehearsing for *L'Illusion* inside the wine-store, 1926.

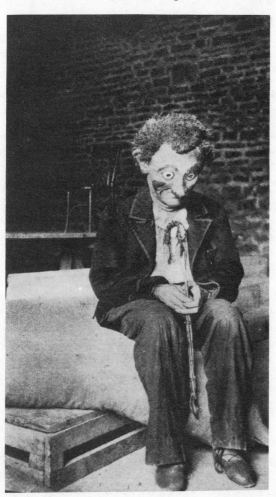

costume (purloined from the wardrobe for *Les Frères Karamazov*) consisting of an old, late-nineteenth-century coat and a pair of mouldy, black–green, baggy trousers "which were so pliable they took on the shape of every move I made". He also found a stick, and an old piece of carpet which, when rolled up, somehow gave the character's gestures more authority.

These four inanimate objects, the coat, trousers, carpet and stick, started my imagination working and began to give shape to my early intuitions of Oscar. This was not happening at an intellectual level; I had no "idea" about Oscar; it was more something I could feel in my bones.[19]

He then went through a period of observation: of a famous political figure, of a night porter at a Swiss hotel they stayed in, as well as examining some memories of his father and also some literary influences – Dostoievsky and Dickens.

bit by bit, I got the idea of the mask I needed and modelled it myself. From the feel of the clothes on my body, from my observation of the politician and the porter and from the mask came my inspiration. With the last-minute addition of a hat, I had equipped my character from head to foot.

It was only at this moment that I could go on to form, more or less intellectually, a conception of Oscar and begin to work on the practical scenarios which would finally lead me to the full realisation of this character.

Oscar was not actually born yet; the birth of a character is a very slow process. All that existed was an embryo, a silhouette. Oscar had some difficulty in speaking because, at this early stage, his existence was based primarily on physical expression. Oscar mumbled for a long time, until his silhouette began to fill out . . .

After all this trial and error – improvising, rehearsing successive scenes, then setting them, and not changing them, except for changes in minute detail and intensity – Oscar Knie was born: naive, vain, sentimental, weak (but imperious when successful), carried to extremes, quick to anger and despair, often drunk, a great talker, full-blooded and, sometimes, obscene.[20]

Dasté's M. César emerged around the same time, and the two grew up together, becoming at times inseparable. Saint-Denis recalls César as "a kind of a dry fish, a sort of Don Quixote, and my Oscar was to become a sort of Sancho Panza, but with much more common sense and a great deal more pessimism. Oscar hated César."

Two limitations in the work method became evident: nearly all the new characters were created by the men in the troupe, and their interaction was hampered by the fact that dialogue did not come naturally to them. A visiting journalist, Jacques Prénat, asked Dasté and Saint-Denis why creative improvisation seemed more difficult for the women in the troupe. Dasté's opinion was that, since improvisation is a sort of trance-state, which requires great physical strength, it was perhaps beyond their powers. It might be added that Copeau may have unwittingly set up the discovery process in specifically masculine terms, requiring the characters to grow up as the result of trial, ordeal and self-assertion. *Le Patron* tried to induce more dialogue with written scenarios in which Knie and César encountered each other. But because the characters had been created by solitary means they were never to achieve the complementary status of, say, Pantalone and Il Dottore. Also, some of the less "grown-up" characters could only appear with them on equal terms provided they remained silent.

None of these problems was insuperable, nor did they prevent intermediate statements of the work in progress being made to the public. In *L'Illusion*, for example, the problem of how to return to the world of the *commedia* was resolved by the device of the play-within-a-play, reminiscent, in one way, of Beaumont and Fletcher's *The Knight of the Burning Pestle*, and, in others, of Pirandello's *Six Characters in Search of an Author* and *Tonight We Improvise*. A youth called Petit Pierre (played by Jean Dasté) joins a company of players to escape the anger of his old father, Beseigne. As soon as he mounts the players' platform, he is considered to be safe: he has left the real world. That platform happens to have been set up in a village called Pernand-Vergelesses . . . Petit Pierre is able to join in since the actors habitually make up their own plays, so he will have no lines to learn. Old Beseigne is in the audience – is their only audience, in fact. He watches his son – in the part of Calixte – fall in love with Melibée and win her (with supernatural assistance). All this happens while Melibée's father, Plébère, is away. When he returns, they do not know how to continue the play. Realising that Beseigne has gone, the actors drop the illusion and argue as to the development of the plot. They have just decided that Plébère should deal with Calixte in a traditionally heavy-handed manner, and the illusion is about to begin again when Beseigne rushes on to the stage, lectures Plébère on the undesirability of parental harshness, and is himself mistaken for an actor by some passers-by. Father and son are reconciled and go home. The make-believe is over, and to show that it was only make-believe, the actors pack up their effects and leave singing their song of the two doves.

Thus Copeau's adaptation offered the Pirandellian view of reality as an illusion, easily contraverted by the statement of illusion as reality. Its genesis obviously owed much to the actual circumstances of rehearsing at the wine store, and the play offered the actors, at base level, the illusion of being at home, no matter where they toured. From then on it was the game that mattered, the interplay between theatre and non-theatre which took place on many levels. On a natural level were the country people (played by Madeleine Gautier, Marguerite Cavadaski, Jean Mercier, Pascal Copeau and Alexandre Janvier), on the supernatural level, Alcandre, the Magician (Jacques Copeau), Sempronio, the Demon (Jean Villard), and the Spirit of Comedy (Suzanne Bing). Another level, the implied one of the whole play as a metaphor for Copeau's relationship to his eponymous company, was also evident:

In *L'Illusion* we have Copeau, played by Copeau. The prologue shows him as he naturally is, the hero of the theatre temporarily cast down, but whose young companions have come to comfort and solicit: they want to act, Copeau shows them how.[21]

Here is that prologue, written by Copeau, as delivered by a figure called the Old Actor, played by Copeau:

26   Jacques Copeau as the Magician in *L'Illusion*.

At the very moment when the curtain rises, actor, you must be ready. That's to say that your appearance, your thoughts and your memory should have been eaten up by the memory, thoughts and appearance of a stranger who is trying to become more present in you than you are yourself. You are not ready unless you have been completely replaced.

Now, imagine that in this struggle the actor, at first overcome by his character, does at last get the upper hand.

Let's suppose that the curtain goes up and the actor isn't ready. Not having had the time to lower his mask, he is taken by surprise. He finds himself discovered, in front of spectators. It has happened to me in my dreams.

What does the actor do? Will he escape into the wings in a single leap? Will he openly assume the illusion by pretending to improvise the actions of his role and pass visibly from being himself into character? Or will he, on the contrary, take a step towards the audience, profit from the mishap and reveal himself to them as he is?

I am sure that no one would believe that he was speaking sincerely. Because people are waiting for him to act, they will think he is acting. You will say that patently he is acting. Well I'm not acting any more. I'm worn out.

On whatever level it was received, *L'Illusion* was a great success, particularly when played to large, receptive audiences on the Copiaus' tours of Europe. *The Times* of 30 November 1928 reviewed a special matinée the previous day at the St James:

What M. Copeau has designed is not a philosophical discourse on theatrical illusion, but *un essai de divertissement ou, comme on dit aujourd'hui, de théâtre pur*. "Pure theatre" – we have had a

27 Suzanne Bing as Célestine, the sorceress, in *L'Illusion*, seated on the *tréteau* inside the wine-store. Mask and costume by Marie-Hélène Dasté.

little of that before, but none so pure, so innocent, that is, of ordinary intellectual coherence, as this, and none, let it be swiftly added, whose innocence has the same charm. M. Copeau's method combines the ease and spontaneity of a good charade with an exquisitely studied accomplishment. He and his company (whose names are not to be identified with the parts they play) have an air of labouring nothing, of arranging and planning nothing, yet there is not an instant in which they are misplaced on the stage, or in which their voices or gestures do not contribute to an elaborate, gentle formalism, which, as if there were such a thing as theatrical good manners, is the basis of their ease. What a humorous villainy lies behind the sorceress's mask! What an eager ingenuousness there is in every tone and movement of the hot-headed youth! What a smoothly inventive elegance distinguishes the performance of M. Copeau himself! Even the devil and the escaped animal provide a careful, laughing decoration in the absurd waving of their legs and tails. You feel, as you watch them all, that they are indeed a community *de famille et d'amité* who are earnestly bent on re-discovering the childhood – or is it the second childhood? – of the theatre. An odd quest that would soon become tedious if pursued at length; but if we must have "pure theatre", may it always come with the grace and polish of Pernand-Vergelesses.

But the times when the young companions could persuade the "worn out" Old Actor to come out of retirement became fewer and fewer. Copeau's presence at Pernand (where the company was supposed to work for eight months in every twelve) became increasingly intermittent. It is worth following the log-book in some detail over his absences, since they reveal what was perhaps the greatest obstacle to the development of the new *commedia* – *le Patron*'s own limited availability. After great successes in Switzerland in 1926 (where Adolphe Appia followed the company's progress with enthusiasm) the company was also well received in Lyon:

In general the press agree on the importance of the dramatic renovation brought about by, and above all presaged by, *L'Illusion*, and the renovation of the Vieux-Colombier in its traditions that have been picked up by the young troupe.
    The troupe returns to Pernand.
    Le Patron and Suzanne Bing go to Paris where they will play on 1 and 6 November at the *Théâtre des Champs Elysées* with the *compagnons de Notre Dame* in *La Vie Profonde de Saint-François d'Assise* by Henry Ghéon.
    Up until 15 November, *Le Patron* gives six dramatic readings and *Le Roi David* . . .
    On 17 November he embarks for New York . . .

(Copeau had been invited to New York to direct *Les Frères Karamazov* at the Guild Theatre, and to undertake a lecture tour.)

2 January, he cables from New York "Success" . . . 6 January he disembarks at Le Havre.

But, instead of picking up the reins at Pernand, there were more readings to be given – in Paris, Switzerland, Belgium and England. Then:

From 11 to 23 February, he is in Geneva, Neuchâtel, Lausanne, La Chaux de Fonds, Zurich.
    He has not yet been to Pernand.

On 25 February he went, but for one night only. After dinner, the company showed him a programme of work they had been engaged in during his absence:

Sunday 26th. *Le Patron* reviews last night's programme and gives his critique. Over and above the dramatic work, there have been great strides in mask-making, singing and in the equipping of the wine store.
    At the end of the visit, Villard brings him the idea, an outline and the music for scenario, *Le Printemps*. This production is the objective of the work until June.
    Try-outs of improvisations and comic scenarios.
    First comic masks.
    A new start made on the search for stock characters.

It was the actors themselves, then, who took up the work on the new *commedia* characters again. Copeau did return in May for a month, but did not become resident as full-time director until 16 June. One reason for his protracted absence was, undoubtedly, financial: the Pernand community depended to a large extent on income from his professional activities. But he also needed, for his own self-esteem, to continue to be recognised as an international figure, an *homme du théâtre*. If the Copiaus had performed more, they could have been more self-supporting, but to have done so would have been increasingly to exploit their actual rather than their potential abilities. This, inevitably, would have meant a greater reliance on the older, former Vieux-Colombier actors, at the expense of the younger, former Vieux-

Colombier School pupils. Copeau had, after all, originally come to Burgundy to run a
new school, not a new company. The core of former pupils, Jean Dasté, Aman
Maistre and Marie-Hélène Copeau did not feel experienced enough to withstand the
impulses of Saint-Denis, Villard and Boverio who, like Dullin and Jouvet before them,
felt that they had careers to get on with. Thus, Marie-Hélène recalls,[22] their style
became a little affected, a little "arch", in order not to have to recognise this potential
dichotomy for what it was.

When Copeau returned, he at once took over the organisation of the weekly and
daily schedule, as well as the direction of *Le Printemps*. In August the log noted:

Rehearsals and preparations, masks, for the show that the young troupe will give in the villages
next January and which will consist of a new mime scenario about vegetation, an improvised
farce where a stock character will be tried out for the first time in public, Michel's one: Knie.

That new piece was eventually entitled *La Danse de la Ville et des Champs* and to the
mime and farce elements were added song, dance and chorus-work (i.e. group
miming and singing).[23] *Le Patron* was again absent throughout its preparation,
returning to the company three days before its première, which was not in January,
but on 4 March 1928 in Meursault. Various friends came from Paris, including two
former Copiaus – Léon Chancerel and Auguste Boverio – and the full house included
also bookers from other regions and important cities.

There were many notable features in this show. The programme announced no list of actors
and their parts; instead it gave a list of scenes and printed the names of the company all in one
group at the end. The whole thing was an intimate collaboration of authorship, acting and
production, and no one person was allowed to predominate in any way. This was emphasised
by a Prologue in which the members of the company were presented to the audience,
displayed their tricks and their properties, and announced that there were *no stars* among
them.[24]

After that Prologue, the play was in three acts, the first of which absorbed the earlier
work done as *Le Printemps*:

Act 1: Winter, the Woodcutters. The awakening of Spring. The Trees. The Wind. The Rain. The
Birds. The Vegetation. The Dance of the Work of Springtime. Jeanne and François. The call of
the town. Entry of the chorus of townspeople. François leaves for the town.

François, a rosy-cheeked Burgundian youth, then becomes bewildered and unhappy
as a result of his experience of the town:

Act 2: The Newspaper Vendor. The arrival of François. The town wakes. François in the
morning in the town. The Machine.[25] The town at work. The Stock Exchange. François leaves
the town. The Beggars. Knie leaves for the country. The Harvesters. The adventures of Knie in
the fields.

Thus Knie, the city-dweller, goes on a counter-pilgrimage, but his adventures are
expressed in farce rather than mime-drama.

Act 3: François *en route* for his home. The menace of the storm. The village chases François. Jean repels François. The Storm. Knie after the storm. The Reconciliation. Knie makes his fortune. Divertissement. Final Chorus.

According to an English spectator, "the coming of the storm over the vegetation, the havoc wrought and the subsequent joy of life reviving were all beautifully symbolised in gesture and attitude".[26] For many of the company the performance was the apotheosis of the ideas it had been working on since the opening of the Vieux-Colombier School in 1920. It used mime, chorus-work, mask-work and . . . new *commedia*. It had the quality of make-believe they had discovered in *L'Illusion*, as well as the celebratory spirit of their occasional festival pieces. Thus they had blended disciplines which they had worked on separately for years and were able to present themselves as that brotherhood united by collective creation which Copeau had so fervently desired. Although it was not a Copeau production (he specifically dissociated himself from it in a programme note), it was, in a vital sense, "school of Copeau". At that first night of *La Danse de la Ville et des Champs*, Villard remembers *le Patron* entering fully into the spirit of the thing:

In the middle of that delirious public, he was laughing, being made sad, clapping like a child. You can imagine whether or not we kept one eye on him! We felt that he was happy and proud of his children. Our joy was complete. We had won the match.[27]

One character at least, as Copeau had predicted years ago, had now grown up, emancipated himself from him and created his own scenario: Knie. As promised, Copeau had allowed his own role as mentor to be subsumed: the time had come for him to revert to his old role as critic. He assembled the company the next day:

We waited for him with incredible impatience! Ready to put our mistakes right, to make our show, on the advice of the master, even more effective. But his face, suddenly, froze our spirits. We were waiting for constructive criticism. Alas, it was a demolition job, total and complete. Copeau was ferocious. All our efforts, all our passions, all our joy – there was nothing left. Nothing found favour in his eyes. His last word, full of a bitter derision worthy of Ecclesiastes was: dust . . .[28]

8   A popular theatre?

The new *commedia* project, the *raison d'être* of the Burgundy community, had evolved empirically into a product that was, somehow, contrary to Copeau's vision. That it did so was due in no small degree to his own increasingly protracted absences. While the father was away, the children played with his tools and spoiled them by using them for a purpose for which they were not intended. Yet it was they themselves who were the very instruments of his craft. By his own disclaimer the product they had fashioned of themselves was theirs, not his. So too, therefore, was its success. There was nothing contrary to the original logic of his scheme in such an eventuality: he had always intended that when the character–children played by the child–characters came of age, he would relinquish his authority over them and allow his function to devolve into that of occasional critic and counsellor. Regrettably, however, any attempt to re-introduce the theory of a continuous, homogeneous progression in Copeau's career founders on the destructive nature of that criticism when given. Whatever his reservations about *La Danse de la Ville et des Champs* (for example, the log-book, written at this time by Suzanne Bing, records that he felt the play to contain the seeds of tragedy rather than comedy), censoriousness as extreme as that reported by Jean Villard-Gilles was bound to lead to further loss of filial respect for directorial authority and parental wisdom. Why adopt such a tone? It seems unlikely that he was jealous of the Copiaus' success, since he himself had always regarded the emotions attending it with suspicion: as early in his practical career as the "rave" reception given to *Les Frères Karamazov* he wrote in his diary:

Success has left me very calm, very much in command of myself, very diffident. Truth to tell, it has left me with a sense of loathing and disgust. Success which one merely exploits, which one merely uses to puff oneself up with vanity and self-advertisement, is nothing, it serves no useful purpose.

Perhaps, then, it was not that he felt the Copiaus' enthusiastic reception to be undeserved, but that he wished to bring them down from their "high", to make their feelings resemble his own self-abnegation in similar, previous circumstances. Perhaps, even, the attack was a displacement activity: he had been far from calm the night before, would perhaps have preferred to be on stage rather than in the auditorium. Was it really himself he wished to censure for sharing their euphoria?

That cry of "dust!", whatever its genesis, marks a point of no return in his progressive estrangement from the group. He later claimed this to be a deliberate response to their sense of needing more freedom and autonomy. They, no doubt, would have said the same of him. The final separation came, rather suddenly, in June

1929. It seems to have been no more planned than the closure of the Vieux-Colombier five years before, since the students (who had been on vacation in May) had been told to re-assemble in July. The company itself now had a reputation (and a repertoire) with which they might have ventured a season in Paris – a home-going which had long been mooted. The introduction of *George Dandin* would extend their Molière range from farce to comedy, *L'Anconitaine* was providing a showcase for their *commedia dell'arte* skills, and they had created (again without Copeau) a new original piece, successor to *La Danse de la Ville et des Champs*, which was agreed to be dramaturgically superior to it. It was called *Les Jeunes Gens et L'Araignée ou La Tragédie Imaginaire* and was based on another scenario by Jean Villard and Michel Saint-Denis. Prior to the closure it had played only nine times (on a European tour in April/May 1929).

The Copiaus' last performance was the reprise of *L'Illusion* which André Obey attended. The floods then receded, but Noah himself stayed in the ark. Some of his charges stayed on at Pernand for a while to be with him, but on 12 October 1929 he noted in his diary:

Michel and Maistre have finally left this morning. My leaves are falling, like the season. Thus reduced, thus disengaged, will I ever re-engage myself? Is it not preferable that I show what I can achieve alone, and perhaps, can I only achieve alone?

Since his conversion to Catholicism, Copeau's need to be alone, to work at his desk alone and even to perform alone, had gradually intensified to the detriment of his desire to direct others. He felt prematurely aged, unable to locate in himself the joy in dramatic creation that had enabled him to collaborate with the young. There had also been too many disappointments along the way, too many times when even his closest collaborators, such as Dullin, had compromised his sense of absolutism and singleness of purpose. As a boy he frightened other children with the intensity of his commitment when playing: they would drop out of a game long before he had exhausted its potential and he would find himself finishing it on his own. Similarly, actors would follow him, but not to the end. But without *le Patron* to provide an intellectual, moral and pedagogical structure, the Pernand community began to slip into superficial "theatrical" behaviour, and lose that sincerity of purpose which validated the naiveté of their performances. During his absences the Copiaus were inclined to "live it up" in a manner reminiscent of the near-rebellion in Morristown: according to Villard, they spent night after night in a café in a nearby village, drinking and entertaining themselves and the locals *ad libendum*. Copeau's return would be marked by his posting notices such as the following (from June 1927):

Time not allocated on the timetable will be employed in drama work: exercises, rehearsals, workshop activities according to the needs of the moment and the requirements of the daily schedule.

Thursday afternoon is intentionally left free, not as time off, but for a *détente*, a chance for individual pursuits, or get-togethers for discussion, reading or, where applicable, listening to a talk or to music. These Thursday afternoons can also be used for domestic chores or personal needs, so that the *whole of Sunday* can be genuinely given over to repose, as it should be.

This schism over the proper relationship between work and leisure activities is indicative not only of a breakdown in communication between Copeau and the Copiaus, but also, perhaps, within Copeau's own psyche. Eric Bentley felt that this attempt to monasticise the creative life was the true chimera of which Gide had spoken: "One suspects that the theatrical impulse to exhibitionism and self-display and the religious impulse to seclusion and self-denial are fundamentally opposite."[1] I prefer to think that these contrary impulses represent a paradox rather than a schism: since the very first season of work at the Vieux-Colombier Copeau had found it impossible to shake off the *bon mot* of one critic who described the work as "The Calvinist Follies". Disaffected pupils at the Vieux-Colombier School charged him with Jansenism and, in Burgundy, whilst ostensibly searching for the new *commedia*, he had, perhaps, been actually attempting to establish the paradox of a public monastery. Finally, Copeau had to admit to himself that it was pointless to continue to cajole and constrain others who, however strong their faith in the theatre, did not want to make a theatre of Faith. They could get on with their own work (and it was important to him that they should do so – hence the introduction of Obey) and he would begin to explore the heart of the paradox – in himself. As well as the new *commedia*, he had always felt the need to develop a new *tragoidia* which would probably need to have roots in personal rather than collective creativity. *La Maison Natale* and *Le Veuf* had been essays in such a genre. Abandoning the "chorus" would now leave him free to go back beyond the flowering of the plays of Aeschylus to the seed of his theatre, to the celebration of divine mysteries by the priest for a massed congregation. The rites would now, of course, be Roman, not Dionysian: theatre as communion would be the quest, not communal theatre.

The ritual preparations for transubstantiation that constitute the Mass admit no lendings from secular dramatics (though the medieval Church did make expeditious use of re-enactment to explicate holy mysteries). For Copeau, the climax of the sacrament was the moment when his opposing impulses became resolved, public performance and spiritual seclusion reconciled. Such a view of Catholic ritual is not heretical. Since the Council of Trent declared that the sacrifice in the Mass is not a repetition of Christ's actual sacrifice, but a bloodless renewal of it, Copeau perceived that in the theatre (where no one dies, either) a kind of communion could also take place. The misguided experiment of *Le Veuf* had, perhaps, been based on such a premise. When he wrote and performed it, his friend Jacques Rivière had just died, unexpectedly. Copeau had spent several days in contemplation of death-bed photographs of the poet before writing a tribute (*Souvenirs d'un Ami*). Rivière's wife, Isabelle, subsequently became a kind of spiritual adviser to Copeau. Another close friend, Henri Ghéon, was instrumental in helping him to an understanding of what a new religious drama could effect in the twentieth century:

Everywhere we feel the need for communion, for getting out of the self, for contemplating the other, communicating with the other. Such exchange is not easy of attainment in the deepening moral and intellectual anarchy. But the desire for it is there, in every group, even the most avant-garde, all claiming some kind of order – Marxist, republican, monarchist, all demanding a society. I do not assert that the theatre can recreate society, but it can help in the work of recreation.[2]

Ghéon, like Copeau, was an adult convert to the faith. Another Roman Catholic playwright, Paul Claudel, was perhaps the most successful in giving dramatic shape to these ideas of theatre-as-communion. While director of the Vieux-Colombier, Copeau had fallen out with Claudel over alterations he wanted made to one of the latter's plays. Early in the existence of the Copiaus, he sought a reconciliation through the intermediary of Isabelle Rivière. This she was soon able to achieve and, in 1925, the two men took up a new correspondence. Shortly afterwards, Copeau made the first of several retreats to a Benedictine monastery. Claudel wrote to him:

Why wait? Being converted is like dying, it does not wait on our convenience. In both cases it is the peace of God which arrives like a thief and He must be obeyed. Just as we happen to be, in our shirt-sleeves.

It is only relevant, here, to follow Copeau's religious quest in so far as it coincided with his theatrical one. After the dissolution of the Copiaus, free at last to meditate, he did no practical work for two years. The timing of the dissolution had, ostensibly, been due to the activities of a pressure group which was bidding to have him put in control of the Comédie-Française. But when he stated his terms to the Ministry of Culture there was silence; for reasons which may never be made clear, the post was then not offered.[3] A plan to re-build the Vieux-Colombier on the original site had previously fallen through and he now also refused Antoine's suggestion that he take over the Odéon. Copeau was emphatic: he had no such thoughts of career, no desire for eminence for its own sake, and, above all, no stomach for a return to the production treadmill that such a position would entail. In so far as one man could, he felt, he had renewed the traditions of theatre and others could now take over that work as, indeed, the "Cartel des Quatre"[4] were already doing. His present hunger was for the theatre of the future, not of the past. Such a theatre, he now believed, must have a sacred function: it was no longer sufficient to set up a "place of refuge" where the talents of the future could multiply – many, in fact, still accused him of having buried them in the soil of Burgundy. Direct experiments needed to be made, presently, in the search for forms that would prove both popular and sacred. But lacking, as he now did, both a theatre and a company, Copeau was not to find many times and places for the sort of work he had in mind.

His first opportunity came for the Florence Festival in May 1933. The piece to be staged was not, in fact, new, but medieval: a fifteenth-century Tuscan mystery play, *Santa Uliva*. The performance conditions were such as to enable Copeau to pull together many of the threads which had been preoccupying him. The production was

28   André Barsacq's design for *Santa Uliva* in the cloister of Santa Croce.

mounted inside a monastery, in the cloisters of Santa Croce. In staging it, Copeau collaborated with André Barsacq, who had recently been working for the Compagnie des Quinze. Copeau had known Barsacq since the latter (at the age of nineteen) had been invited by Dullin to design *Volpone* for him at the Théâtre de l'Atelier in 1928. Barsacq subsequently designed a permanent staging for the Atelier that was an acknowledged descendant from the Vieux-Colombier. Now he was to work with *le Patron* himself for the first time:

At his side, with twenty years between us, I discovered what had given value to his initiative, his teaching and his example, I discovered sincerity in hard work, the savour of honesty and probity in theatrical expression placed in the service of poetry.[5]

They seated the audience on three sides, rather than using the single, narrow, presentational face of the Vieux-Colombier stage, thus giving Copeau as director a chance to compose sculpturally rather than pictorially. Otherwise his treatment of this non-theatre space was entirely consistent with his previous *mises en scène*. The cloister is rectangular and they seated the audience in the arcades. In the centre, around the walls, they erected a *tréteau* with a forestage and another platform on either side, further forward, with two walkways joining them to the middle of the centre stage.

Thanks to this very simple device we were able to arrive at a scenic hierarchy: all the important scenes took place on the central platform, subordinate scenes on the subsidiary stages.[6]

The large cast moved all over the playing area as changes of place and time required.

Paradise was situated on the first-floor level. Settings and properties also used the elemental, indicative style of the Vieux-Colombier: a king in his throne room would be denoted by having him mount the central platform accompanied by two standard-bearers. On a subsidiary stage, a scene in an inn was created by one inn-keeper and one stool.

Thus the scenic architecture was determined by the existing architecture of the playing space: no concrete was needed, since marble was already *in situ*. The director's job, to which Copeau responded with all his old enthusiasm, was to find a natural sympathy between the locales afforded by the holy space and the rhythms of the sacred text. He was, however, concerned over the possible reaction of a sophisticated Italian audience to the rather theatrically naive play that was being revived for them:

It must be said that throughout the rehearsal period and right up to the first performance of *Santa Uliva*, we were surrounded by pretty deep scepticism. This old Mystery Play which I could be seen to be taking so seriously seemed destined to be ridiculed by the Florentine public, which, I was informed is the sharpest and most critical in Europe. Well, when my two Angels fought with the Devil in the vast enclosure of Santa Croce, not so much as a breath could be heard.

"If only you could have seen", he wrote to Suzanne Bing, "the actors launch themselves across the open space and on to the playing area, and the décor of the scenes move with the drama." Open space had roused his appetite: from now on he would feel limited working "within three walls".

But the principal development in Copeau's thinking at this time was not to do with spatial dimension, whether in or out of a theatre building, nor with the relationship between play and playing space. These considerations were prefigured in his earlier work: only the circumstances had changed. It was the overtly religious subject-matter of *Santa Uliva* that reflected not only his new quest for theatre-as-communion but also the related consideration of the actual popularity of theatre. As he later put it:

The nature of the audience, its quantity, its disposition, that indeed is the essential primary given factor in the problem of theatre. We did not understand it very well until today, but we did have a presentiment of it, some thirty years ago, when we tried to restore the impulse towards dramatic presentation. That is why we made such an effort to attract, re-unite and give satisfaction to a new audience. But since our ambition was to re-fashion everything and to remain unsullied in doing so, it was important for us to avoid commercial pressure as much as possible, and so we took refuge in small-scale theatres . . . I can understand today that those little theatres were only technical laboratories, conservatoires where the noblest traditions of the theatre could be resurrected, but which could not be called true theatres, because they lacked a true audience.[7]

But now Copeau felt that there would be no point in re-building a popular theatre unless it was also a religious one, and vice versa. The function of theatre was to reveal the roots of social morality and to connect them to the growth of contemporary human behaviour. He agreed with Ghéon that modern man was alone, isolated from his fellows, and that to be socially and morally regenerative, theatre would have to accept as a root either Christianity or Marxism. After the performances of *Santa Uliva* he wrote to an Italian friend:

I had a vivid impression in Florence that Catholic theatre could undergo a renaissance. All technical questions are more or less pointless . . . *Uliva* has had a great importance for me. You will perhaps appreciate why later.[8]

Copeau's next practical opportunity was not until the Florentine May Festival two years later. This time the play to be presented was *Savonarola* by Rino Alessi, with music by Mario Castelnuovo Tedesco. The play was new, but unfortunately Copeau found it "very mediocre". He was glad to have the "tireless" help of André Barsacq once more, since he himself was recovering from an operation. The setting was to be the Piazza della Signoria, where Savonarola was actually burned at the stake in 1498. Seating was installed for 4,000 people – the back row rose to 23 m above ground level. Again there was multiple staging, a singing choir, an orchestra and a speaking chorus. The crowd scenes were so populous that Copeau was obliged to direct them

29   *Savanarola* in the Piazza della Signoria, Florence, 1935.

from the top of one of the four lighting towers. Barsacq describes the scene:

When the people of Florence were called to arms, the trumpeters mounted the central platform and sounded the alarm. Then, from every side, we had the crowd arrive through the tunnels situated under the grandstands. A mixed crowd of every hue which swarmed into the square and finally assembled in blobs of colour, yellow, green, red, blue. A remarkable sight. All accompanied by music and spoken choruses. The different playing spaces lit up as their turn came and again, through the miraculous effect of these historic locations, the whole effect had a real sense of grandeur.

A rich palette . . . an early essay in *son et lumière* . . . something had affected Copeau's sense of dramatic asceticism, and in his last major theoretical work, *Le Théâtre Populaire*, he was at pains to show that he was aware of the dangers of working with spectacle on such a scale:

even when mystically orientated, the theatre must not follow the example of spectacular displays which would over-extend its capacities. One must be careful not to confuse that which belongs to the parade and the festival procession with that which is essentially dramatic. Theatre for the masses does not have to be mass theatre.[9]

As he wrote that seminal work, the social and cultural integrity of his country was, for the second time in his life, being undermined by war. A national theatre, he believed, would have a vital part to play in national regeneration. For this task it would need to be truly popular: its antecedents would be the theatres of classical Greece and the Middle Ages, "two forms of dramatic representation which have their point of origin in the moral life of the people, and their repercussion on it. Both these forms imply a stable view of humanity, of its origins, its actuality, its relationship with the Almighty."[10]

It seems that his nomination for the directorship of the Comédie-Française had stayed on the table. He actually took over there in 1940, but, given his ideas on the regenerative power of a national theatre, it is hardly surprising that he fell out with the Vichy authorities and returned to Pernand early in 1941.[11] He wrote in his diary:

Return to reality after eight months spent among the ghosts in that monument to vanity and *cabotinage*, the Comédie-Française. How much richer the world becomes when one regains the freedom to offer one's heart to it. Fortunately the vanities which sustain mankind do not have much sway over me. How easily they fall away!

In 1943, Copeau was able to return to the medieval form for what was to be his last major production: *Le Miracle du Pain Doré*, a play commissioned to commemorate the five hundredth anniversary of the foundation of the Hospices de Beaune. This time the text was neither old nor new, but Copeau's favourite combination of the two: an original play re-worked by himself. *Le Miracle du Pain Doré* is by Copeau, after a fourteenth-century play, *Pierre le Changeur, Marchand*. From the physical point of view the performance conditions were similar to those at Santa Croce: the courtyard of the Hospice resembles a rectangular cloister. Copeau and Barsacq used only one quarter of it, more or less a square formed by the angle of two sides and an

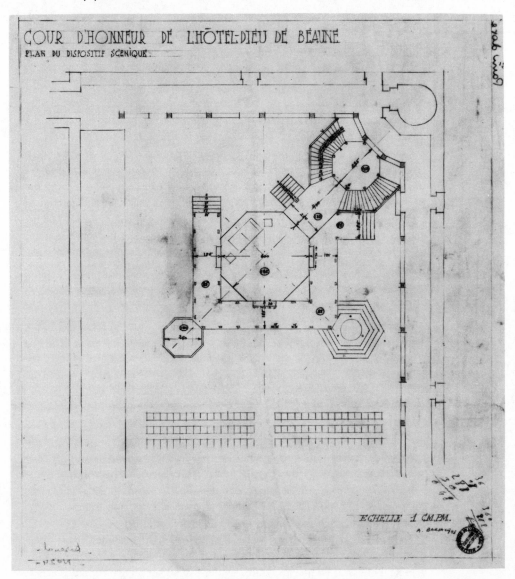

30 André Barsacq's design for *Le Miracle du Pain Doré* in the courtyard of the Hospice de Beaune, 1943.

architectural feature in the yard: a well which they used to represent hell. This formed the downstage right corner of the playing area, as seen by the spectators. Devils leapt from its curb-stone on to the first downstage platform, which was horseshoe-shaped. A higher platform, octagonal in shape, was enclosed by the horseshoe and connected upstage by two flights of stairs to a turret projecting from the galleries supporting the roof. This turret was situated right in the corner of the courtyard and was used to represent the heavens. On either side, at the same height, the deambulatories contained chorus, choir and orchestra, as used in *Santa Uliva* and *Savonarola*.

Copeau's use of these supplementary disciplines in his "late" open-air religious productions stemmed from his reading of Appia and from the experiments in Greek tragedy and Japanese Noh which had been made at the Vieux-Colombier School. But their application now, he stressed, was not a matter of technical experimentation or formal predilection: the two types of *choeur* (choir and chorus in English) and the musical accompaniment were intended to give the action a spiritual dimension, the harmonics which Appia had sought between dramatic action and musical duration:

a dramatic idea requiring musical expression in order to be revealed must spring from the hidden world of our inner life, since this life *cannot be expressed* except through music, and music can express only that life. By means of the spoken word, the dramatist endows it with a practical dramatic form and composes the poetic–musical text, the *score*; this text imposes an already living role upon the *actor*, a role he has now only to take on. The proportions of this role determine the form of the setting through *three-dimensionality* (the point of contact between the living actor and the inanimate setting); the nature and extent of the three-dimensionality determine the *spatial arrangement* of the setting ... This hierarchy is organically composed: music, the soul of the drama, gives life to the drama, and by its pulsations determines every motion of the organism, in proportion and sequence.[12]

Copeau was himself no musician, but had become convinced that music was a part of the vocabulary of dramatic art, not merely an adjunct to it: Appia's hierarchy might even be the correct one. During his retreats to the Benedictine monastery of Solesmes he had learnt to appreciate the dramatic power of the Gregorian chant and now, in *Le Miracle du Pain Doré*, he was able to collaborate with a musician who was well-versed in the monodic and polyphonic music of the fifteenth and sixteenth centuries, Joseph Samson, the Master of the Chapel at the Cathedral of Dijon.

The speaking chorus, on the other hand, was intended to be an intermediary rather than an evocative instrument, both commenting and commentating, capable of varying both its role and its voice. In the manner of its Greek and Japanese antecedents, it could change both tense and voice, sometimes speaking, sometimes chanting, from a position in relation to the action that was sometimes subjective, sometimes objective. Unlike the choir, which was placed behind the spectators, so as not to distract them, the chorus was significantly visible. Its flexible, intermediary position somewhere between master of ceremonies and medieval fool bore some resemblance to the roles which Copeau himself tended to adopt — often perhaps as a convenient resolution of the difficulties of the director/actor dichotomy. In *Le*

Miracle du Pain Doré, he again cast himself as Le Meneur du Jeu, thus adding, as it were, a Chorus to the chorus. Jean Dasté played the part of Pierre le Changeur and Marie-Hélène Dasté designed and made the costumes. On returning to Pernand, Copeau noted in his diary:

It was really, I think, a model for a religious celebration, as beautiful as *Santa Uliva* in Florence, in the same line, but with more resonance and, perhaps, more discipline.

Then, after a few days for reflection:

there I really got out of the theatre, out of any purely aesthetic considerations. There I found a coherent milieu: the kindness of the Charitable Sisters, the gathering together of a modest company that I had not found myself but that had been nurtured by Jean [Dasté] who I myself had nurtured; the collaboration of those whose work had for so long been harmonised with mine, and to whom I had been faithful and who had remained faithful to me: Maiène, Jean, Barsacq . . .[13]

To sum up, then: working outdoors on a large scale with a small core of trusted collaborators, Copeau was successful in bringing out the values of a religious text which he himself had adapted. In order to do so he created compositions using large numbers of actors, multiple naked stages, music and choruses that both sung, spoke

31   *Le Miracle du Pain Doré*, Act 3, scene 3. Jean Dasté, left, as Pierre le Changeur.

and chanted. He was able, in fact, in the present, to satisfy many of the conditions he had set out for a popular sacred theatre of the future. The question of an audience for it could not be permanently resolved in war-time. The occasion of the performances of *Le Miracle du Pain Doré* was a well-attended celebration of a place of healing in a town with which he himself had personal associations as a result of the many visits of the Copiaus. Although a "one-off", it was this sentiment (which had necessarily been missing in the Florentine productions) which gave him a rare sense of satisfaction, of having achieved something that was not "dust". "Those two days", he wrote to Suzanne Bing, "were extraordinarily harmonious . . . it seemed to me to be a model sacred celebration and the crowning of what we have been doing for twenty years in this area . . . The town was a little uplifted by a calm, caring exaltation, in between the pealing of the bells, which was translated into modest, but heartfelt testimony . . . It must be followed up: I am thinking of the twelfth centenary of the death of Saint Benoît which could be celebrated at Solesmes in four years time . . ."

But, by 1947, Copeau's health was so impaired by the long-term effects of atherosclerosis that the project was never seriously begun. For years the nature of his illness was not understood by Copeau himself, or by his doctors. He once confided to Michel Saint-Denis that the first presentiments he had of it were in 1924, and that they had contributed to his decision to give up the direction of the Vieux-Colombier and the pressures that it involved. In 1941, whilst staying with Roger Martin du Gard, he collapsed completely, was hospitalised, but seemed quickly to recover. The state of medical knowledge was such that his condition was not diagnosable. His Pernand diaries are full of complaints about fatigue, of sensing his mental powers to be diminished, interspersed with periods of good health, of feeling in control of his faculties and intending to "start again".

It is, then, possibly churlish to point out that in singling out three productions from a period of over twenty years, I have, in this chapter, perhaps attributed a coherence to Copeau's life and work which is not borne out by an examination of the rest of his activities. During this time, as well as editing, writing and lecturing, he was also directing on a freelance basis and some of the commissions that he accepted[14] could have offered at best a journeyman's sense of a job well done. On a chance encounter in Paris, Saint-Denis watched his uncle at work on a play and commented that he did not recognise him in what he was doing. "Moi non plus", was Copeau's reply. One senses that, at times, he was working for the sake of working, keeping his name on the posters whilst looking for a new major phase to his career that never came.

Much of the time he was no longer sure that he wanted to be a theatre director anyway. He had always wanted to write a major work and had even toyed with the idea of an autobiographical novel, a kind of French *My Life in Art*. Since the Vieux-Colombier days, his literary friends, sensing that he was lost to the kind of theatre they had envisaged together, had been encouraging him to consider making his next important contribution to theatre through writing rather than directing. As has been noted in *La Maison Natale* and *Le Veuf*, Copeau's inclination as a writer of original plays was towards self-exposition; similarly, when he was directing, he found it difficult to keep off the stage himself. One should not characterise him, however, as an egotist, any more than, say, Strindberg: an ego-burner, rather. Copeau's sense of dedication to his chosen medium is reminiscent of the Arab saying that "a teacher burns down so that others may see". Such missionary purpose was to find its final dramatic working out in his play *Le Petit Pauvre*, based on the life of St Francis of Assisi. It was published in 1946, but never staged during Copeau's lifetime.

He finished writing *Le Petit Pauvre* in 1942, but it was not performed until 1950, the year after his death, in the market-place of the village of San Miniato. The director was one of his latter-day pupils, Orazio Costa. Marie-Hélène Dasté told me that it was faithfully interpreted, on a wooden platform that her father would have owned to . . . It could, perhaps, be considered therefore as his fourth open-air religious production. *Le Petit Pauvre* embodies many of the stylistic importations of the other three productions, in particular the use of a Greek-style chorus. On 11 June 1941 Copeau read the first act to his wife, Agnès. She told him that she found it "magnificent". In his diary he recorded her judgement with a certain vehemence:

I can write, then, create, make an opus, which is the only thing in which I can henceforth find any satisfaction.

That he should need to boost himself in the privacy of his own journal in such a way is perhaps sufficient testimony to the fact that he found creative writing a slow, circumspect business. The doubts cast by the failures of *La Maison Natale* and *Le Veuf* had left him with a need to test every scene and every line over and over against his own sense of dramatic probity. Copeau was once accused of knowing too much about acting to make a successful actor. It is probable that he was also too aware of the art of writing for the theatre to make a successful playwright. Nevertheless, Clement Borgal, in his authoritative biography *Jacques Copeau*, asks us to consider *Le Petit Pauvre* as Copeau's last testament, arguing it to be a play, like Claudel's *Christophe Colomb*, which plays better than it reads. In Borgal's opinion, the slight disguise offered for Copeau's own life is the play's strength, not its weakness:

FRANCIS (to Bernard):   My order and my testament are very simple, clear things. You need only to understand them in the same clear and simple manner, and to practise them right up until the end . . . you see, I am at the last extremity of my life, and am still looking at the beginning. That's what I have always done. That's what I recommend to you: always look at the beginning . . .

Since *Le Petit Pauvre* is a kind of ending, it is, I think, important that Copeau should not be remembered for it. Unless someone can prove otherwise (and it would have to be done by putting on his plays rather than writing about them), Copeau's efforts to become a writer remain so. "His drama was that he always wanted to be a dramatist", was Marie-Hélène Dasté's conclusion to her discussions with me. Louis Jouvet perceived that the drama was acted out, not in his plays, but in Copeau's work as a director:

Copeau is a dramatist. It is just that, apart from a few rare attempts, he expressed himself through the daily practice of directing and creating his own theatre.

He sacrificed his career as a playwright to undertake the renovation of the art of theatre for his own epoch, and everyone working in theatre today is in some degree indebted to him.

"Whatever I do this winter", he wrote to me in 1920, "with the plays that I am about to put on, and though they turn out to be marvels of direction and interpretation, it will only be a miserable travesty of my thinking. As to this thinking itself, I am unable to truly express it. I grope after it, and can sometimes touch it without seeing it."[15]

The two main models for Copeau in his (secular) quest were Stanislavsky and Molière: it cannot be argued that he was as good an actor as either, nor as great a writer as the latter. Some might wish he had never attempted to act or write, but had concentrated on developing his gifts as a director. But it is precisely his personal appetite for all the contributory arts of theatre that distinguished his work as a *metteur en scène*. In a true ensemble there are specialists, but no specialisation. The only way that Copeau knew how to teach that fact was by example, not once, but repeatedly. In order to do so, new beginnings had continually to be sought, even at the expense of premature endings. Also new acolytes were often needed, since his actor–children constantly grew up and left him, finding that to practise for themselves the "simple, clear things" that he had preached, it was necessary to remove themselves from his presence. There is no doubt that that presence could be overwhelming, absolute in its demands for respect. In 1918 he wrote to Jouvet:

When you are with me you are in the right, our work lives and prospers, it all holds together, it all works. When you are not with me, you are in the wrong, our work decays, nothing works. Because I am the boss, because I carry everything inside myself, because everything depends on me. In me, and in as much as I am accepted, recognised, helped and seconded by my collaborators, most of all by you – recognised and seconded *blindly*. When I say blindly, I do not mean at all in the sense of servitude, nor of belittling the personalities which surround me. I require, I am calling for a free development of our community, of our communion. But you can only communicate *in me*, "in the bosom of the Father". Don't smile at these mystical expressions . . . you would never smile at them if you once really understood with what a sombre passion I uphold my ideal, with what true modesty, in what spirit of sacrifice, including that of my life . . . I am now at an age where the work to be accomplished counts before all else.[16]

Four years later, when Jouvet felt himself to be of a similar age, continued collaboration on *le Patron*'s terms became impossible.

Today, Copeau's demanding presence is no longer an obstacle, but neither do we have the opportunity to learn from (and through) him at first hand. That is where books come in. This one is offered as a simple primer, a beginner's guide to what *le Patron* began.

Appendix
Chronological list of Copeau's productions

1913/14 (Vieux-Colombier, Paris)

October 23	*Une Femme Tuée par la Douceur*, adapted by Copeau and Croué. *L'Amour Médecin*, Molière.
November 11	*Les Fils Louverné*, Jean Schlumberger.
November 18	*Barberine*, Alfred de Musset.
November 23	*L'Avare*, Molière.
November 24	*Le Pain de Ménage*, Jules Renard. *La Peur des Coups*, Georges Courteline.
November 29	*Jeu de Robin et de Marion*, Adam de la Halle.
December 22	*La Farce du Savetier Enragé*, adaptation of anonymous play by Alexandre Arnoux.
January 1	*La Jalousie du Barbouillé*, Molière.
January 15	*L'Echange*, Paul Claudel.
February 7	*Le Testament du Père Leleu*, Roger Martin du Gard. *La Navette*, Henri Becque.
March 10	*Les Frères Karamazov*, adapted by Copeau and Croué.
April 23	*L'Eau de Vie*, Henri Ghéon.
March 19	*L'Avare* (reprise), *Le Carosse du Saint-Sacrement*

1917/18 (Garrick, New York)

November 27	*Impromptu du Vieux-Colombier*, Jacques Copeau. *Les Fourberies de Scapin*, Molière.
December 5	*La Navette* (reprise), *La Jalousie du Barbouillé* (reprise). *Le Carosse du Saint-Sacrement*, Merimée.
December 11	*Barberine* (reprise), *Le Pain de Ménage* (reprise).
December 25	*La Nuit des Rois* (reprise).
January 8	*La Nouvelle Idole*, François de Curel.
January 23	*Les Frères Karamazov* (reprise).
January 31	*La Surprise de l'Amour*, Marivaux.
February 6	*La Traverse*, Auguste Villeroy. *Poil de Carotte*, Jules Renard.
February 20	*Les Mauvais Bergers*, Octave Mirbeau.
March 5	*La Petite Marquise*, Meilhac and Halévy. *L'Amour Médecin* (reprise).
March 19	*L'Avare* (reprise), *Le Carosse du Saint-Sacrement*
April 2	*La Paix Chez Soi*, Georges Courteline. *Le Testament du Père Leleu* (reprise).
April 16	*La Chance de Françoise*, Georges de Porto-Riche.

1918/19 (Garrick, New York)

October 14	*Le Secret*, Henry Bernstein.
October 21	*Le Mariage de Figaro*, Beaumarchais.
October 28	*Blanchette*, Eugène Brieux.
November 4	*Georgette Lemeunier*, Maurice Donnay.

125

November 11   *Crainquebille*, Anatole France. *Le Voile du Bonheur*, Georges Clemenceau.
November 18   *La Femme du Claude*, Alexandre Dumas, fils.
November 25   *Le Médecin Malgré Lui*, Molière. *Gringoire*, Theodore de Bonneville.
December 2   *Rosmersholm*, Ibsen.
December 9   *Le Gendre de M. Poirier*, Emile Augier.
December 16   *Les Caprices de Marianne*, Alfred de Musset. *Le Fardeau de la Liberté*, Tristan Bernard.
December 23   *Les Romanesques*, Edmond Rostand.
December 30   *Boubouroche*, Georges Courteline. *L'Enigme*, Paul Hervieu.
January 6   *L'Avare* (reprise).
January 13   *Chatterton*, Alfred de Vigny.
January 20   *Les Frères Karamazov* (reprise).
January 27   *Le Menteur*, Corneille.
February 3   *L'Ami Fritz*, Erckmann-Chatrian.
February 10   *Pelléas et Melisande*, Maurice Maeterlinck.
February 17   *Washington*, Percy Mackaye. *La Coupe Enchantée*, La Fontaine and Champmeslé.
March 3   *La Veine*, Alfred Capus.
March 17   *Le Misanthrope*, Molière.

1919/20 (Vieux-Colombier, Paris)

February 10   *Le Conte d'Hiver*, adapted by Copeau and Suzanne Bing.
March 5   *Le Pacquebot Tenacity*, Charles Vildrac. *Le Carosse du Saint Sacrement* (reprise).
April 10   *L'Œuvre des Athlètes*, Georges Duhamel.
April 27   *Les Fourberies de Scapin* (reprise)
May 27   *Gromedyre-le-Vieil*, Jules Romains.
July 1   *Phocas le Jardinier*, Francis Vielé-Griffin. *La Folle Journée*, Emile Mazaud. *La Coupe Enchantée* (reprise).

1920/21 (Vieux-Colombier, Paris)

October 15   *Le Médecin Malgré Lui* (reprise).
October 17   *La Folle Journée* (reprise).
October 19   *La Coupe Enchantée* (reprise). *Le Pain de Ménage* (reprise).
October 27   *La Surprise de l'Amour* (reprise). *La Jalousie du Barbouillé* (reprise).
November 5   *Phocas le Jardinier* (reprise)
November 29   *Le Pacquebot Tenacity* (reprise). *Le Carosse du Saint-Sacrement* (reprise).
December 22   *La Nuit des Rois* (reprise).
December 29   *Les Fourberies de Scapin* (reprise).
January 24   *Le Pauvre sous l'Escalier*, Henri Ghéon.
March 23   *La Mort de Sparte*, Jean Schlumberger.
April 15   *Oncle Vania*, Chekhov.
May 13   *La Dauphine*, François Porche.
May 27   *L'Amour Médecin* (reprise). *Un Caprice*, Alfred de Musset. *Le Testament du Père Leleu* (reprise).

1921/1922 (Vieux-Colombier, Paris)

October 15	*Au Petit Bonheur*, Anatole France. *La Fraude*, Louis Fallens.
October 25	*Le Mariage de Figaro*, Beaumarchais.
October 29	*Le Testament du Pere Lèleu* (reprise).
November 3	*La Navette* (reprise).
November 6	*Un Caprice* (reprise).
November 30	*Les Frères Karamazov* (reprise).
December 5	*La Nuit des Rois* (reprise).
December 19	*Cromedeyre-le-Vieil* (reprise).
January 6	*Le Médecin Malgre Lui* (reprise). *Le Pain de Ménage* (reprise).
January 25	*Le Misanthrope*, Molière.
February 26	*La Jalousie du Barbouillé* (reprise).
March 7	*L'Amour, Livre d'Or*, Alexis Tolstoy (adapted by de Gramont). *La Mort Joyeuse*, Nicholas Evreinov (adapted by Denis Roche).
March 11	*L'Avare*, Molière.
March 13	*La Coup Enchantée* (reprise).
April 10	*Le Pacquebot Tenacity* (reprise).
April 21	*Les Plaisirs du Hazard*, René Benjamin.
June 16	*Saul*, André Gide.

1922/1923 (Vieux-Colombier, Paris)

October 14	*Le Mariage de Figaro* (reprise).
October 15	*Le Carosse du Saint-Sacrement* (reprise). *Le Pacquebot Tenacity* (reprise).
October 16	*Un Caprice* (reprise). *Le Testament du Père Leleu* (reprise). *Le Pain de Ménage* (reprise).
October 25	*Sophie Arnould*, Gabriel Nigond. *La Pie Borgne*, René Benjamin. *La Belle de Hagueneau*, Jean Variot.
November 15	*Le Menteur* (reprise). *Maître Pierre Pathelin*, adapted by Roger Allard.
November 22	*Les Plaisirs du Hazard* (reprise).
December 6	*Le Misanthrope* (reprise).
December 14	*La Nuit des Rois* (reprise).
December 21	*Michel Auclair*, Charles Vildrac.
February 2	*La Princesse Turandot*, by Carlo Gozzi, adapted by J.-J. Olivier.
March 8	*Prologue Improvisé*, Jacques Copeau. *Le Médecin Malgré Lui* (reprise). *Un Caprice* (reprise).
March 22	*Le Misanthrope* (reprise). *La Coupe Enchantée* (reprise).
March 28	*Dardamelle*, Emile Mazaud.
April 4	*La Folle Journée*, Emile Mazaud.
May 15	*Bastos le Hardi*, Léon Regis and François de Veynes.

1923/1924 (Vieux-Colombier, Paris)

October 31	*L'Imbécile*, Pierre Bost. *La Locandiera*, Carlo Goldoni (adapted by Mme. Darsenne).
November 8	*Bastos le Hardi* (reprise).

November 21   *Le Testament du Père Leleu* (reprise). *La Pie Borgne* (reprise). *La Folle Journée* (reprise).

December 18   *La Maison Natale*, Jacques Copeau.

January 3   *Le Misanthrope* (reprise).

February 14   *Il Faut que Chacun soit à sa Place*, René Benjamin.

April 3   *Le Pacquebot Tenacity* (reprise). *Le Carosse du Saint-Sacrement* (reprise).

1925–1929 (Repertoire of the Copiaus)

1925

January 24   *L'Impôt*, Jacques Copeau.

January 24   *L'Objet*, Jacques Copeau.

May 17   *Le Veuf*, Jacques Copeau.

May 17   *Les Sottises de Gilles*, Thomas de Guelette.

May 17   *Les Jeunes Filles à Marier*, Léon Chancerel.

May 24   *Mirandoline*, adapted from Goldoni's *La Locandiera* by Copeau.

August 15   *Le Médecin Malgré Lui*, Molière. *Arlequin Magicien*, Jacques Copeau.

August 23   *Les Vacances*, Michel Saint-Denis.

October 25   *Les Cassis*, adapted from Lopé de Rueda by Copeau.

October 25   *L'Ecole des Maris*, Molière.

November 14   *Fête de la Vigne et des Vignerons*.

November 14   *La Coupe Enchantée*, La Fontaine and Champmeslé.

1926

January 24   *La Pie Borgne*, René Benjamin.

October 3   *L'Illusion*, Jacques Copeau from Fernando de Rojas and Pierre Corneille.

1927

November 8   *L'Anconitaine*, Jacques Copeau from Ruzzante.

1928

March 4   **La Danse de la Ville et des Champs*, Jean Villard-Gilles and Michel Saint-Denis.

1929

April 27   **Les Jeunes Gens et L'Araignée*, Jean Villard-Gilles and Michel Saint-Denis. *George Dandin*, Molière, and *La Surprise de L'Amour et du Hazard*, Beaumarchais, were rehearsed but never performed.

1932–1939

1932

November 10   *Jeanne*, Henri Duvernois, Th. des Nouveautes, Paris.

1933

June 5   *Santa Uliva* at the Maggio Fiorentino.

1934

April 30   *Persephone*, André Gide. L'Opéra, Paris.

October 11   *Rosalinde* (adapted from *As You Like It*). L'Atelier, Paris.

1935

May 28   *Savonarola*, Rino Alessi. Maggio Fiorentino.

1936

March 7   *Beaucoup de Bruit pour Rien (Much Ado About Nothing)*. Théâtre de la Madeleine, Paris.

November 10   *Napoléon unique*, Paul Raynal, Porte St Martin, Paris.

December 7   *Le Misanthrope*, Molière. Comédie-Française.

1937

January 28   *Le Trompeur de Seville*, André Obey. Porte Saint-Martin, Paris.

May 24   *Bajazet*, Racine. Comédie-Française.

November 22   *Asmodée*, de Mauriac. Comédie-Française.

1938

June 1   *Come vi Piace (As You Like It)*. Florence.

November 21   *Le Testament du Père Leleu*, Martin du Gard. Comédie-Française.

1940 (as Director of the Comédie-Française)

September 8   *Le Misanthrope* and *Un Caprice*.

October 14   *Le Pacquebot Tenacity* and *Le Carosse du Saint-Sacrement*.

November 11   *Le Cid*, Corneille.

December 23   *La Nuit des Rois*.

1943

July 21   *Le Miracle du Pain Doré*. Hospice de Beaune.

* Productions from which Copeau specifically dissociated himself. There were a number of other occasional pieces created by the Copiaus, as well as prologues and medleys of songs.

Notes

All quotations in the text from Copeau's Diaries are from the originals which are part of the Fonds Copeau at the Bibliothèque de l'Arsenal. These are, however, currently being prepared for publication by Claude Sicard.

1. Dramatic renovation

1. An Ironworks at Raucourt (Ardennes).
2. *Le Théâtre Populaire*, first published in the collection "Bibliothèque du Peuple", PUF, Paris, 1941. Reprinted in *Jacques Copeau, Registres I*, texts collected and established by Marie-Hélène Dasté and Suzanne Maistre Saint-Denis (Gallimard *NRF*, Paris, 1974), pp. 277–313.
3. *Essais, Antée, le Théâtre, le Figaro illustré, le Gaulois, le Petit Journal*, etc.
4. From one of the lectures that Copeau delivered (in English) during his stay in America, entitled "To the Playhouse". Subsequently published in *The Playhouse* (Cleveland, Ohio), no, 3, 1918–19.
5. 1932, article in *Les Nouvelles Littéraires*, reprinted in *Jacques Copeau, Registres I*, pp. 87–91.
6. Waldo Frank, *The Art of the Vieux-Colombier* (*NRF*, NY and Paris, 1918).
7. An exaggeration. That he knew next to nothing of Meyerhold's work was revealed to him in December 1916 when he read *The Path of the Modern Russian Stage* and *Theatre Unbound* by Alexander Bakshy.
8. Jacques Copeau, "An Essay on Dramatic Renovation", reprinted in *Registres I*, pp. 19–32.
9. "If the French theatre is dying, it is the professionals who are killing it . . . One should not blush about being an amateur. One should freely welcome the artist, however great, who never ceases, in the course of his career, being an amateur, if one gives the word its proper sense of *one who loves*. He who gives himself to his art, not through ambition, nor through vanity, nor through cupidity, but through love alone, and who, subordinating his entire being to such pure passion, makes a vow of humanity, of patience and courage." (Extract from an article, "Pour les Amateurs", first published in *L'Est Dramatique*, 4 November 1925, quoted in *Registres I*, pp. 145–6).
10. Jacques Copeau, "Conference aux Annales", 1933, lecture extract in *Registres I*, pp. 37–41.
11. *Ibid*, p. 35.
12. "An Essay on Dramatic Renovation" in *Registres I*, p. 23.
13. Introduction to Berthold Mahn, *Souvenirs du Vieux-Colombier* (Claude Aveline, Paris, 1926).
14. "An Essay on Dramatic Renovation" in *Registres I*, pp. 31–2.
15. Jacques Copeau, *Souvenirs du Vieux-Colombier* (Nouvelles Editions Latines, Paris, 1931), pp. 19–21.
16. Georges Duhamel, *Le Temps de la Recherche* (Paul Hartman, 1947), pp. 219–20.
17. Article in the *New York Times*, 28 January 1917.
18. Paul Albert Laurens.
19. Roger Martin du Gard, *Souvenirs Autobiographiques et Littéraires*, quoted in *Jacques Copeau, Registres III, Les Registres du Vieux-Colombier*, texts collected and established by Marie Hélène Dasté and Suzanne Maistre Saint-Denis (Gallimard *NRF*, Paris, 1979), p. 118.
20. Introduction to Mahn, *Souvenirs de Vieux-Colombier*.
21. Interview with the author, 4 March 1983.
22. Jean Villard-Gilles, *Mon Demi-Siècle* (Lausanne, 1954).
23. *Ibid*.
24. Frank, *The Art of the Vieux-Colombier*.
25. Michel Saint-Denis, *Training for the Theatre* (Theatre Arts, NY, and Heinemann, London, 1982), p. 34.
26. Published in the same year (1931) – not to be confused with Mahn's earlier book of the same name.
27. Copeau, *Souvenirs du Vieux-Colombier*, pp. 35–40.

28. Copeau later had actors rehearse under their breath: particularly in comedy he found this brought lightness and clarity of tone, as well as comedic intensity.
29. "Ma dette envers Copeau" in Roger Martin du Gard, *Œuvres Complètes, I* (Gallimard, Paris, 1955), pp. 72–3.

2. The text

1. Regis Gignoux, "Une Chartreuse de Comédiens" (*Le Figaro*, 25 August 1913).
2. Georges Duhamel (in *Mercure de France*, 14 August 1913).
3. See bibliography.
4. 15 December 1913.
5. Extract from a lecture given in 1922, quoted in *Jacques Copeau, Registres II*, texts assembled and presented by André Cabanis (Gallimard NRF, Paris, 1976), p. 22.
6. Extract from a lecture given in 1933, quoted in the catalogue of the exhibition: *Jacques Copeau et le Vieux-Colombier* (Bibliothèque Nationale, Paris, 1963).
7. Quoted by Denis Gontard in the introduction to his edition of *Le Journal de Bord des Copiaus* (Seghers, Paris, 1974), p. 23.
8. *Ibid.*
9. Jean Villard (later Jean Villard-Gilles), *La Chanson: le Théâtre et la Vie* (Mermod, Lausanne, 1942), p. 40.
10. Pronounced "Co-pee-ass".
11. Copeau, *Souvenirs du Vieux-Colombier*, p. 120.
12. Norman Marshall, *The Producer and the Play* (MacDonald, London, 1957), p. 62.
13. Interview with the author, 13 July 1984.
14. Saint-Denis, *Training for the Theatre*, p. 34.
15. Translated in Cole and Chinoy (eds.), *Directing the Play* (Bobbs-Merrill, Indianapolis and NY, 1953), pp. 148–59.
16. *Ibid*, p. 151.
17. Jessmin Howarth, cited in Norman Henry Paul, "Jacques Copeau, Apostle of the Theatre" (Ph.D. dissertation, New York University, 1961).
18. This attitude can lead to obsession. Jouvet, while working alternately with Georges Pitöeff as director at the Comédie des Champs Elysées, came to regard the writer as the sole dramatic creator. He took infinite care to discover the author's intentions and to interpret them with absolute fidelity. This painstaking determination to give full value to each line made every one seem of equal weight and significance, to the point where the meaning of the play became smothered in its own words. Copeau, realising that Jouvet's development as a director was becoming stultified as a result, wrote to him urging him to use his own ideas to "fertilise with new capital the traditions you have inherited from us".
19. Villard-Gilles, *Mon Demi-Siècle*.
20. Saint-Denis, *Training for the Theatre*, p. 30.
21. Cole and Chinoy (eds.), *Directing the Play*, p. 150.
22. *Ibid.* p. 152.
23. Copeau, *Souvenirs du Vieux-Colombier*, p. 159.

3. The enemy of the theatre

1. Copeau applied to Heineman for the translation rights, but a French version had already been commissioned.
2. Quoted in J. Chiari, "Jacques Copeau", *World Review* (Jan.–June 1952), p. 38.
3. Copeau's first experience of the role of director. He did consider taking on the part of Ivan himself, and later regretted not having done so.
4. Meyerhold, quoted by Edward Braun, *Meyerhold on Theatre* (Methuen, 1969), p. 122.
5. Copeau, diary entry.
6. Copeau, quoted by Henri-Pierre Roche in "Arch Rebel of French Theatre Coming Here" (article in *New York Times*, 28 January 1917).

7. Copeau, *Souvenirs du Vieux-Colombier*, pp. 79–80.

8. Letter to Alfred Cortot quoted in *Jacques Copeau, Registres IV*, texts collected and established by Marie-Hélène Dasté and Suzanne Maistre Saint-Denis (Gallimard *NRF*, Paris, 1984), pp. 165–6.

9. Roche, *New York Times*, 28 January 1917.

10. Copeau, "An Essay on Dramatic Renovation", in *Registres I*, p. 29.

11. Interview with the author, 14 July 1984.

12. Marie-Hélène Copeau, Notebook 1921/2 (unpublished, extract translated by Barbara Anne Kusler "Jacques Copeau's Theatre School: L'Ecole du Vieux-Colombier, 1920–29" (Ph.D. thesis, University of Wisconsin, 1974), pp. 164–5).

13. Jacques Copeau, Diary (unpublished): extract quoted in *Jacques Copeau/Roger Martin du Gard, Correspondence* (Gillimard *NRF*, Paris, 1972), vol II, p. 688.

14. I have rendered some sections of this prospectus in full, others in title only. We have already noted, for example, Copeau's later objections to eurythmics.

15. "Why do you persist in calling actors, my actors in particular, *cabots*? You forget that, in as much as I have placed myself among them, lived their life, shared their work, it has been precisely so that they should no longer be called cabots, nor considered as such . . ." (Copeau, letter to Jean Schlumberger, 9 August 1919, published in *Revue d'Histoire du Théâtre*, no. 4. October 1963, pp. 382–5).

16. Saint-Denis, *Training for the Theatre*, p. 31.

17. Notebook, August 1918.

18. Notebook, May 1918.

19. Quoted in *Notes sur le Métier de Comédien*, notes taken from the diary and writings of Jacques Copeau by Marie-Hélène Dasté (Michel Brient, Paris, 1955), p. 47.

20. Marque had sculpted a bust of Molière for the opening of the Vieux-Colombier in New York.

21. Marie-Hélène Dasté, interview with the author, 14 July 1984.

22. Marie-Hélène Copeau, Notebook 1924, quoted by Kusler, "Jacques Copeau's Theatre School", p. 117.

23. Maurice Kurtz, *Jacques Copeau, Biographie d'un Théâtre* (Paris, 1951), p. 65.

24. Copeau, *Souvenirs du Vieux-Colombier*, p. 99.

25. Zeami's *Kwadensho*, quoted by Arthur Waley, *The Nō Plays of Japan* (Allen and Unwin, 1921), p. 28.

26. Saint-Denis, *Training for the Theatre*, p. 33. He exaggerates his collaboration in the work of the school: both he and Boverio and Villard (all later to be key members of Les Copiaus) were no more than interested observers of the work of the Vieux-Colombier School.

27. Copeau, *Souvenirs du Vieux-Colombier*, pp. 99–100.

28. Marie-Hélène Copeau, Notebook 1924, quoted and translated by Kusler, "Jacques Copeau's Theatre School", p. 150.

4. The naked stage

1. Copeau, "To the Playhouse".

2. Kenneth MacGowan and Robert Edmond Jones, *Continental Stagecraft* (Benn Brothers, London, 1923), p. 171.

3. *Ibid.* p. 172.

4. *Ibid.* p. 173.

5. Saint-Denis, *Training for the Theatre*, p. 27.

6. Jouvet somehow managed to study architectural drawing whilst in the trenches.

7. Copeau, *Le Théâtre Populaire*, reprinted in *Registres I*, pp. 271–313.

8. Diary, 8 October 1916.

9. For a full discussion of Craig's Scene, see Christopher Innes, *Edward Gordon Craig*, in this series.

10. Antonin Raymond was a young architect appointed at Copeau's insistence in preference to Edward Margolies who had converted the Bijou. Unfortunately his lack of seniority meant that certain entrepreneurs, who wanted to use the building as a cinema when the French Theatre left, were constantly going behind his back and getting the builders to follow Margolies' original plans.

11. *Registres IV*, p. 127.

12. Appia had been collaborating with Dalcroze for ten years and taught at his institute.

13. *Registres I*, p. 67.

14. Saint-Denis, *Training for the Theatre*, p. 27.

15. Marshall, *The Producer and the Play*, p. 157.

16. Cole and Chinoy (eds.), *Directing the Play*, p. 157.

17. With the exception of Vienna, where they visited the Redoutensaal of Marie Theresa, "converted by the Austrian Government into a theater without proscenium, machinery or scenery. Audience and actors are lit by crystal chandeliers and surrounded by Gobelins and a permanent setting of baroque architecture. Mozart and Reinhardt bring to it an old and a new theatricalism."

18. MacGowan and Jones, *Continental Stagecraft*, p. 99.

19. *Ibid.* p. 100.

20. *Ibid.* p. 104.

21. *Ibid.* pp. 104–5.

22. *Britannicus* was announced for the 1913/14 season, but was never produced. Copeau mooted the idea of a chamber theatre devoted to the work of Racine, where the small size of the auditorium, enhanced by wooden walls, would let the human voice resonate like a string quartet. The only Racine play that he did direct was *Bajazet* for the Comédie-Française in 1937.

23. Marshall, *The Producer and the Play*, p. 60.

24. *Ibid.* p. 60.

5. Two presentations

1. Solidity was the hallmark of the indicative pieces that Jouvet added to the permanent setting: "A detail that shows the working of his mind is to be found in the screens he uses to create a room in *Les Frères Karamazov*; by giving them two or three inches of thickness and a certain amount of molding, he has escaped the impression of the bare, the unsubstantial, and the untheatrical, which the screens of other designers produce" (MacGowan and Jones, *Continental Stagecraft*, p. 174).

2. "La Mise en Scène au Vieux-Colombier", *Art et Décoration*, October 1923, pp. 113–22.

3. MacGowan and Jones, *Continental Stagecraft*, p. 178.

4. Adolphe Brisson, *Feuilleton du Temps*, 8 March 1920.

5. Quoted by Michel Saint-Denis, *Training for the Theatre*, p. 30.

6. Claude Roger-Marx, "Conte d'Hiver", *Comoedia Illustre*, 15, March 1920.

7. Ludmila Savitzky, "Charles Vildrac", *Choses du Théâtre*, no. 14, February 1923.

8. *Ibid.*

9. Roger-Marx, "Conte d'Hiver".

10. Notes taken by Louis Jouvet at a public class at the Vieux-Colombier School, 30 March 1921, published in *Mise en Scène des Fourberies de Scapin* (Editions du Seuil, Paris, 1950), pp. 30–1.

11. *Registres II*, pp. 40–1.

12. *Jacques Copeau/Roger Martin du Gard, Correspondence*, vol. II, pp. 832–3.

13. For the Vieux-Colombier School; see note 10 above.

14. For the opening performance in New York it was backed by two cloths specially painted by Bonnard.

15. In his lectures, Copeau enthused about the ancestor of his *"tréteau nu"*, the four square trestles with half-a-dozen planks across, used in the theatre of Lopé de Rueda, as described by Cervantes.

16. Frank, *The Art of the Vieux-Colombier*, p. 142.

17. Saint-Denis, *Training for the Theatre*, p. 29.

18. Again one is struck by the similarity with Brecht's ideas on staging. However, I know of no direct connection between this production and that of, say, the 1927 "Little" *Mahagonny*.

19. Jacques Copeau, "Quelques indications sur des representations de Molière aux Etats-Unis", *Revue de Littérature Comparée*, 2, April/June 1922, pp. 280–2.

20. Jouvet, *Mise en Scène des Fourberies de Scapin*, p. 17.

21. *Ibid.* p. 24.

22. This argument is taken from an article by Copeau, *"Les Fourberies de Scapin"*, reprinted in *Registres II*, pp. 291–8.

23. *Ibid.* p. 297.

24. Jouvet, *Mise en Scène des Fourberies de Scapin*, pp. 112–20.

25. Time was so short, they even rehearsed another play on the boat going over.

26. Jouvet, in his 1949 production of *Scapin* at the Théâtre Marigny, with Jean-Louis Barrault as Scapin and Pierre Barthin as Géronte, did make use of the umbrella once more.
27. Quoted by Jouvet, *Mise en Scène des Fourberies de Scapin*, p. 154.

6. Retreat in Burgundy

1. Quoted and translated by Eric Bentley, "Copeau and the Chimera", *Theatre Arts Monthly*, January 1950, 24, no. 1, p. 50.
2. *Ibid.* p. 50.
3. "The Solitude of Jacques Copeau", *The Dublin Review*, no. 225, Summer 1951, pp. 83–112.
4. Quoted by Marcel Doisy, *Jacques Copeau, ou l'Absolu dans L'Art* (Le Cercle du Livre, Paris, 1954).
5. *Le Théâtre Indiscrét de l'An 1924 par?* (Georges Crès, Paris, 1925), p. 222.
6. *Ibid.* pp. 222–3.
7. The rule-book for a Benedictine community. One would have thought a map might have been a more useful companion to have on his knees while driving round the Côte d'Or, but the *Règle* was Copeau's spiritual guide in what he was about to do.
8. Copeau, *Souvenirs du Vieux-Colombier*, p. 106.
9. *Ibid.* p. 71.
10. Gontard (ed.), *Le Journal de Bord des Copiaus*, pp. 45–6.
11. Notebook entitled "Livre des Fêtes de l'Ecole du Vieux-Colombier 1922–3", kept by Clarita Stoessel, quoted by Kusler, "Jacques Copeau's Theatre School", p. 165.
12. In fact Dasté was delayed and came on the next morning by train, so the welcome was given to Copeau who arrived that same evening from Paris, where he had been giving a lecture on the Russian theatre.
13. Villard-Gilles, *Mon Demi-Siècle*, p. 115.
14. Chancerel had been Copeau's secretary for the last season at the Vieux-Colombier. After leaving Les Copiaus he went on to found his own companies: Les Comédiens Routiers and Le Théâtre de l'Oncle Sebastien, as well as setting up *La Revue de l'Histoire du Théâtre* and being instrumental in the spread of drama activities in French youth organisations.
15. On the other hand Chancerel was not adding anything to the troupe's range: he had modelled himself so closely on *le Patron*, even down to the adoption of a similar pipe, that he could never have been a contributor to the kind of relationship that Copeau had had with Dullin and Jouvet. To a lesser extent the same problem of over-emulation also beset Michel Saint-Denis.
16. Villard-Gilles, *Mon Demi-Siècle*, p. 118.
17. Copeau's mother, Hélène, Michel Saint-Denis' father, Charles, and Copeau's friend, the poet Jacques Rivière, had all died within a few weeks of each other.
18. A geometric pattern was marked out on the floor as an aid to blocking.
19. Villard-Gilles, *Mon Demi-Siècle*.
20. Jacques Prénat, "Visite à Copeau", *Latinite* (December 1930).
21. Whilst on a trip to Florence, the wife of the painter van Rysselberghe found a reproduction of the pair of doves engraved on a flagstone in the church of San Miniato in Tuscany. They became the logo of the Vieux-Colombier, then of Les Copiaus and of La Compagnie des Quinze. Copeau called them "our allusive arms" (heraldic arms in which the charge makes a pun on the name of the bearer).
22. Copeau, *Souvenirs du Vieux-Colombier*, pp. 118–19.

7. The new *commedia*

1. I have translated "comédie nouvelle" as "new *commedia*" in order to avoid confusion with Greek New Comedy.
2. Copeau, *Registres II*, p. 76.
3. Copeau, Diary, 1916.
4. André Gide, *Journal (1889–1935)* (NRF, Paris, 1939), vol. I, p. 529.
5. One of these friends was probably Roger Martin du Gard. Copeau mounted his farce of peasant life *Le Père Leleu* in 1914. Subsequently Martin du Gard accompanied the Vieux-Colombier Company on

their tour of England. He developed his own allied idea of a *comédie des trétaux* with fixed characters: M. and Dame Punais (a physically and financially well-padded couple), Fric and Miette, a pair of sly valets, Monsieur Malandrin, a gangster, and so on.

"I wanted them to be recognised as soon as they leapt on to the *tréteau*. I persuaded myself that they would quickly be as popular as Polchinelle, Arlequin, don Quichotte or Monsieur Prudhomme; and I already envisaged, with the assistance of Copeau, composing a series of short satirical comedies for the Vieux-Colombier, in which we would together have lightly castigated the misdemeanours of our contempories and the morals of our time." (Martin du Gard, quoted by Denis Boak in his *Roger Martin du Gard* (Oxford, 1963), p. 183.)

Unlike Copeau, he could envisage the finished product very clearly. But Copeau knew what stood between his writer friend's conception and any practical execution of it. He later wrote that Martin du Gard ". . . began to dislike this too human instrument, this medium which was too exposed to weakness and accident, which sooner or later escapes from the strict control of the artist, whose work it deforms and betrays. He wanted to keep everything in his own hands and let nothing slip from them." (*Ibid.* p. 183).

(For a full statement of Martin du Gard's ideas for a new *commedia* see his "Notes sur la 'Comédie de Trétaux'" (October 1917) in *Jacques Copeau/Roger Martin du Gard, Correspondence*, vol, I, pp. 819–25.

6. Dasté collection. This notebook will be published in a future *Registre*.
7. *Ibid.*
8. Lecture given by Copeau, "Le Théâtre dans le Monde", at Coppet on 17 September 1935.
9. See Pierre Louis Duchartre, *The Italian Comedy* (Harrap, 1929), pp. 299–301 for a full account of Dullin's *commedia* troop entertainments.
10. Copeau, letter to his wife Agnes, published in *Registres III*, p. 319.
11. Copeau, notebook, quoted in *Registres III*, p. 322.
12. His ward, Madeleine Gautier, became a member of the company. Of his actual children, Pascal gave occasional performances but wanted to pursue his studies rather than an acting career. Edwige (Edi) helped with the décors, but was eventually to become a nun. Marie-Hélène (Maïène) later married Jean Dasté. Bernard Bing (Copeau's son with Suzanne Bing) later became a member of the Comédiens Routiers before also joining a religious Order. Copeau's family were thus as divided as himself between Theology and Thespianism.
13. Copeau, letter to his wife, published in *Registres III*, p. 321.
14. This art of *pantomime* (not to be confused with English Christmas pantomimes) has, of course, been resurrected and developed, first of all by Copeau's pupil, Etienne Decroux (who acknowledges an enormous debt to him in his *Paroles sur la Mime*, Gallimard, Paris, 1963) and then by Jean-Louis Barrault, Marcel Marceau *et al.*
15. Kusler, "Jacques Copeau's Theatre School", quoting Marie-Hélène Copeau and other contemporary accounts.
16. Léon Chancerel, notes in the margin of Doisy's book on Copeau, quoted by Gontard (ed.), *Le Journal de Bord des Copiaus*, p. 29.
17. Prénat, "Visite à Copeau".
18. Letter to Copeau, June 1928, quoted by Kusler, "Jacques Copeau's Theatre School", p. 208.
19. Saint-Denis, *Training for the Theatre*, pp. 177–8.
20. *Ibid.* pp. 178–9.
21. Review in the Genevan edition of *Comœdia*, 25 October 1926.
22. Interview with the author, 13 July 1984.
23. This style of performance was, of course, based on experiments made in the Vieux-Colombier School. A description of ensemble choral presentation from the School may help in envisioning the techniques of *La Danse de la Ville et des Champs*: in one improvisation, fishermen's wives were waiting on the shore for news of a shipwreck:

"A group of pupils come to the front of the stage. They must produce, despite their masked faces, a vision of a strand and of fisher-folk peering out into the stormy sea. Their bodies create not alone their own emotion but by a subtle fugue the heave of the water. A rowboat comes up. It is created by two actors in a rhythmic union of propulsion. They leave their boat and mount the stairs to the apron. They have news of the drowning of a comrade: the news transfigures the group. The scene shifts to what is an interior of a fisher cottage. The wife and the children await the master. The friends come in with the tragic tidings." Waldo Frank, "Copeau Begins Again", *Theatre Arts Magazine*, September 1925.

24. Phyllis Akroyd, *Dramatic Art of the Compagnie des Quinze* (Eric Partridge, 1935), pp. 20–1.

25. "I have a vivid recollection of how they presented machinery in mime to symbolise industrialism" (*ibid.*). This exercise, like so many that were devised by Bing and Copeau, has become a standard in the drama workshop repertoire.

26. *Ibid.* pp. 21–2.

27. Villard-Gilles, *Mon Demi-Siècle*, pp. 142–3.

28. *Ibid.* p. 143.

8. A popular theatre?

1. Bentley, "Copeau and the Chimera", p. 50.

2. Henri Ghéon, *The Art of the Theatre*, trans. by Adele M.Fiske (Hill & Wang, NY, 1961), p. 76. (I am indebted to Linda Modyman de Vries' Ph.D. thesis, "The influence of Jacques Copeau on the actor training theories of Michael Saint-Denis" (University of California, Los Angeles, 1973) for pointing out the effect on Copeau of Ghéon's ideas about theatre-as-communion.)

3. The last entry in the Copiaus' log reads: "Jacques Copeau has been pressed from several directions: would he accept the post of Administrator-General of the Comédie-Française? His reply is that he will not press his candidature against those of other candidates, but if the Minister does call on him to re-organise the House of Molière, he will accept, given certain provisions concerning length [of contract] and freedom of action.

4. Louis Jouvet, Charles Dullin, Georges Pitöeff, and Gaston Baty.

5. Quoted in André Barsacq, *Cinquante Ans de Théâtre* (Exhibition Catalogue, Bibliothèque Nationale, Paris, 1978), p. 16.

6. André Barsacq, *Communication au Centre d'Etudes Philosophiques et Techniques du Théâtre*, quoted by Clement Borgal in *Jacques Copeau* (l'Arche Editeur, Paris, 1978), p. 256.

7. Copeau, *Le Théâtre Populaire*, reprinted in *Registres I*, p. 285.

8. Letter to Silvio d'Amico, 5 August 1943, quoted by Borgal, *Jacques Copeau*, p. 260.

9. Copeau, *Le Théâtre Populaire*, reprinted in *Registres I*, p. 301.

10. *Ibid.* p. 279.

11. He was also suspected of being in communication with his son, Pascal, who was active in the Resistance.

12. Adolphe Appia, *Music and the Art of Theatre*, trans. Robert W. Corrigan and Mary Douglas Birks (University of Miami Press, 1962), p. 139.

13. This syndrome, of the success of the ensemble leading to its dissolution into the enhancement of individual careers, is either a cause or an effect of European theatre's continued domination by the "star system". Joan Littlewood, of Theatre Workshop, wrote in her obituary on Harry H. Corbett: "For me it has been a bitter pill to swallow. So many beautiful clowns type-cast in their dull brothel, the endless repetition of the act, and the spurious success which kills." Copeau, at least, saw Dullin and Jouvet achieve a status equal to his own as passionate directors and teachers, and many of his actor alumni pursue separate disciplines with a dedication that he must have approved of, much as he may have deplored their separatism in itself.

14. The 1934 production of *Rosalinde* (based on *As You Like It*) at the Atelier should be exempted from this criticism: in it Copeau once again showed his facility for creating "tableaux" which evoked the atmosphere of Shakesperean comedic locales while using a minimum of décor.

15. Jouvet, *Mise en Scène des Fourberies de Scapin*, p. 17.

16. Quoted *Registres IV*, p. 325.

Select Bibliography

Copeau's own writings on theatre, whether previously published or not, are being edited as a series of *Registres*:

I: *Appels.* Paris 1974.
II: *Molière.* Paris 1976.
III: *Les Registres du Vieux-Colombier I.* Paris 1979.
IV: *Les Registres du Vieux-Colombier II. America.* Paris 1984.

Further volumes are in preparation. Major works on Copeau in French include:
Borgal, Clement. *Jacques Copeau.* Paris 1960.
Doisy, Marcel. *Jacques Copeau, ou l'Absolu dans l'Art.* Paris 1954.
Gontard, Denis (ed.). *Le Journal de Bord des Copiaus.* Paris 1974.
Kurtz, Maurice. *Jacques Copeau, Biographie d'un Théâtre.* Paris 1951.

There are no monographs on Copeau in English, but here is a select list of works which include extended references and articles which deal with specific aspects of his theatre:
d'Amico, Silvio. "The Play of St. Uliva", *Theatre Arts Monthly*, New York, September 1933, pp. 681–5.
Bentley, Eric. *In Search of Theatre.* New York, 1959.
    "Copeau and the Chimera", *Theatre Arts Monthly*, January 1950, pp. 48–51.
Frank, Waldo. "The Art of the Vieux-Colombier", *Salvos*, New York, 1924, pp. 119–67.
    "Copeau Begins Again", *Theatre Arts Monthly*, September 1929, pp. 585–90.
Katz, Albert M. "The Genesis of the Vieux-Colombier", *Educational Theatre Journal*, December 1967, pp. 433–46.
    "Jacques Copeau, The American Reaction", *Players Magazine*, February 1970, pp. 113–43.
    "Copeau as Régisseur, an Analysis", *Educational Theatre Journal*, May 1973, pp. 160–72.
Kusler Leigh, Barbara. "Jacques Copeau's School for Actors", *Mime Journal*, nos. 9 and 10, 1979.
MacGowan, Kenneth and Edmond Jones, Robert. *Continental Stagecraft.* New York, 1922.
Mambrino, Jean. "The Solitude of Jacques Copeau". *The Dublin Review*, 225, 1951, pp. 83–112.
Saint-Denis, Michel. *Theatre, The Rediscovery of Style.* London, 1960.
    Training for the Theatre, New York & London, 1982.
    "Modern Theatre's Debt to Copeau", *The Listener*, 16 February 1950.

Two important works by Copeau that have been translated into English are:
"An Essay on Dramatic Renovation", in *Actors on Acting*, Cole and Chinoy (eds.), New York, 1949.
"On Dramatic Economy", in *Directing the Play*, Cole and Chinoy (eds.), New York, 1953. (Re-published as *Directors on Directing*, 1963.)

For a complete biography see:
Paul, Norman H. *Bibliographie – Jacques Copeau.* Paris 1979.

Index

Aeschylus, 25, 26–7, 28, 113
Albane, Blanche, 10, 14, 18
Alessi, Rino, 17, 129
Allard, Robert, 18, 61, 127
Amour Médecin, L', 34, 125
Anconitaine, L', 29, 95, 112, 128
Antoine, André, 4, 13, 27, 60, 70, 90, 114
Appia, Adolphe, 2, 58–9, 108, 120
Arlequin, 96, 97, 103
Arlequin Magicien, 28, 90, 91, 95, 102
Arnoux, Alexandre, 26
Artaud, Antonin, 8, 28
Athénée St-Germain, Théâtre de l', 8, 53
Avare, L', 12, 125, 126, 127

Bacqué, André, 69, 75
Barsacq, André, 115, 117–19, 121
Bataille de la Marne, La, 30
Bataille, Henri, 3, 7
Becque, Henry, 25, 125
Bentley, Eric, 83, 113
Bergson, Henri, 5, 6, 27
Bing, Bernard 84
Bing, Suzanne, 34, 84, 87, 88, 101, 108, 111, 116, 122, 126; actress 9, 16, 17, 18, 30, 105, 107; teacher 42, 48, 49, 93
Blum, Léon, 1
Bossu, Michette, 84, 87
Bouquet, Romain, 17, 18, 75
Boverio, August, 84, 85, 87, 88, 101, 109
Brecht, Bertholt, 62
Brighella, 72
Brook, Peter, 34
Brothers Karamazov, The, 1, 6, 10; see also *Frères Karamazov, Les*
Brouillard du Matin, 27

Camus, Albert, 50
Cariffa, Antoine, 18
Carosse du Saint-Sacrement, Le, 34, 60, 61, 64, 68, 125, 126, 127, 128, 129
Cassis, Les, 29, 92, 128
Cavadaski, Marguerite, 84, 87, 90, 105

Chancerel, Léon, 84, 87, 88–9, 101, 102, 109, 128
Chennevière, Georges, 84
Claudel, Paul, 10, 26, 49, 114, 125
Colombine, 96, 97
Comédie-Française, 4, 29, 38, 72–3, 77, 114, 118, 129
Commedia dell'arte, xiv, 71, 81, 92, 95, 96, 101, 102, 112; see also Arlequin, Brighella, Colombine, Dottore, Pantalone, Pierrot, Scappino, Tartaglia
Compagnie des Quinze, La, 29, 30, 35, 102, 115
Conte d'Hiver, Le, 60, 126
Cooper, Claude, 61
Copeau, Agnès, 84, 123
Copeau, Edi, 84, 87, 90
Copeau, Marie-Hélène, 84, 87, 88, 109; see also Dasté, Marie-Hélène
Copeau, Pascal, 84, 88, 105
Copiaus, Les, 29, 88, 89, 91–4, 101, 102, 109, 111, 112, 113, 114, 122
Corneille, 29, 128, 129
Costa, Orazio, 123
Courteline, Georges, 25, 125, 126
Craig, Edward Gordon, 2, 4, 13, 36, 37–9, 44, 46, 55, 56
Cromedeyre le Viel, 34, 126
Croué, Jean, 10, 72, 125

Dalcroze, Emil Jacques, 38–40, 42, 43, 58
Danse de la Ville et des Champs, La, 109–12, 128
Dasté, Jean, 84, 87, 88, 91, 102, 103, 104, 121
Dasté, Marie-Hélène (Maïène), 14, 15, 42, 103, 105, 109, 121, 123; see also Copeau, Marie-Hélène
Decroux, Etienne, xiii, 84
Desjardins, Paul, 7
Dorcy, Jean, 84
Dottore, Il, 102, 105
Duhamel, Georges, 10, 14, 64, 126

Dullin, Charles, xiii, 8–9, 11, 12–13, 32, 37, 40, 42, 62, 97, 112, 115
Durec, Arsène, 7, 8, 37
Duse, Eleanora, 36, 37

Ecole des Maris, L', 93, 128
Euripides, 25
Eurythmics, 38–41, 48, 58

Femme Tuée par la Douceur, Une, 14, 62, 125
Fête de la Vigne et des Vignerons, 92
Fils Louverné, Les,
Fort, Paul, 4, 27
Fourberies de Scapin, Les, 34, 63, 72–81, 95, 125, 126
Frank, Waldo, 16, 43, 73
Fratellini, Les, 97, 98, 99, 101
Frères Karamazov, Les, 8, 36, 52, 60, 61, 104, 108, 111, 126; *see also Brothers Karamazov, The,*

Galli, Yvonne, 84, 87
Gallimard, Gaston, 14, 53
Garrick Theatre, New York, 39, 54, 56, 59, 72, 73, 74, 125–6
Gautier, Marie-Madeleine, 84, 88, 105
George Dandin, 112, 128
Ghéon, Henri, 27, 49, 82, 95, 113, 127, 128
Goldoni, Carlo, 28, 90, 127
Grant, Duncan, 15
Granville Barker, Harley, 4, 33–4, 49

Hevesi, Alexander, 36
Heywood, Thomas, 25; *see also Une Femme Tuée par la Douceur*
Howarth, Jessmin, 39

Ibsen, Henrik, 25, 27, 82, 126
Illusion, L', 29, 94, 95, 105–7, 108, 112
Impôt, L', 85, 86, 128
Impromptu de Versailles, L', 72
Impromptu du Vieux-Colombier, L', 72, 125
Inès, Denis d', 72
Irving, Sir Henry, 38

Jalousie du Barbouillé, La, 34, 125, 126
Janvier, Alexandre, 84, 125
Jeunes Filles à Marier, Les, 89, 128
Jeunes Gens et l'Araignée, Les, 112

Jolson, Al, 60
Jones, Robert Edmond, 51–2, 60–2, 68
Jordaan, Catherine, 68, 69
Jourdain, Francis, 53, 54
Jouvet, Louis, xiii, 81, 84, 99–100, 123, 124; actor 11, 12, 17, 18, 19, 20, 21, 75, 76, 77, 78, 80; designer 54, 56, 57, 58, 59, 65, 68; lighting designer 15, 68–9

Kabuki theatre, 61
Kahn, Otto, 41
Kantan, 49

Lascaris, Theodore, 15, 125
Loire, 30
Lory, Jane, 17
Lugné-Poë, Aurélien-Marie, 4, 22, 27

MacGowan, Kenneth, 51–2, 60–2, 68
Maison Natale, La, 27–8, 82, 90, 113, 128
Maistre, Aman, 84, 87, 88, 91, 109, 112
Maistre, Suzanne, 84, 109
Marque, Albert, 46
Marshall, Norman, 62–3
Martin du Gard, Roger, 13, 23, 41, 68, 72, 82, 83, 85, 122, 125, 129
Médecin Malgré Lui, Le, 81, 90, 126, 128
Merimée, Prosper, 25, 64, 65, 125; *see also Carosse du Saint-Sacrement, Le*
Meyerhold, Vsevelod, 4, 37, 92
Miracle du Pain Doré, Le, 118–21, 129
Mirandoline, 28, 90, 128
Misanthrope, Le, 34, 77, 126, 127, 128, 129
Molière, 10, 25, 26–7, 28, 31, 34, 56, 63, 81, 90, 93, 95, 99–100, 101, 112, 124, 125, 127, 128, 129; *see also Amour Médecin, L'; Ecole des Maris, L', Fourberies de Scapin, Les, George Dandin, Impromptu de Versailles, L', Jalousie du Barbouillé, La, Médecin Malgre Lui, Le, Misanthrope, Le*
Musset, Alfred de, 10, 25, 126

Noé, 29, 30
Noh drama, 48–50, 62, 95, 120; *see also Kantan*
Nouvelle Revue Française, La (NRF), 1, 3, 6, 26, 41, 50, 53, 64, 83, 95

Nuit des Rois, La, 1, 15–23, 34, 55, 60, 87, 125, 126, 127, 129